10-68   69
                         99
                        120
                        149

WIZARDS THAT
PEEP AND
MUTTER

WIZARDS THAT PEEP AND MUTTER

Christians and Superstition

And when they shall say unto you, Seek unto them that have familiar spirits, and unto wizards that peep, and that mutter: should not a people seek unto their God?
Isaiah 8:19

PAUL BAUER

FLEMING H. REVELL COMPANY
WESTWOOD, NEW JERSEY

U.S.A.
FLEMING H. REVELL COMPANY
WESTWOOD, N.J.

LONDON
MARSHALL, MORGAN AND SCOTT, LTD.
1-5 PORTPOOL LANE
HOLBORN, E.C.1

AUSTRALIA
117-119 BURWOOD ROAD
MELBOURNE, E.13

NEW ZEALAND
24 EMPIRE ROAD
EPSOM, AUCKLAND

SOUTH AFRICA
P.O. BOX 1720, STURK'S BUILDINGS
CAPE TOWN

Translated by Hadyn Barnes from the original
German *Horoskop und Talisman* published by Quell-Verlag, Stuttgart.
Published in Great Britain under the title *Christianity or Superstition*
by Marshall, Morgan & Scott, London; and published in the U.S.A.
under the title *Wizards That Peep and Mutter* by Fleming H. Revell
Company

Preface

SUPERSTITION has reached a high-water mark today. It resembles a club which is split up into numerous denominations. It manifests itself in a vast number of ways: esoteric clubs, occult circles, reading clubs for the study of periodicals and books, clienteles of magicians, clairvoyants and astrologers. It has created whole industries and does a flourishing trade in pseudo-scientific apparatus. The faithful are found equally among the simple folk and the intellectuals. It penetrates the sober world of politics and the Stock Exchange. The number of those who adhere to a belief in spirits and the stars, who seek advice about their future from cards or coffee dregs, or their medical help from pendulum diviners and spellbinders, who expect the world to be saved by flying saucers or entertain all sorts of other ideas and counsels, goes into millions in Germany alone. There are no statistics, but the number of those who belong to this "Church" of superstition probably exceeds the number of believing Christians. It is so in Germany and will not be otherwise in other countries.

People may be astonished that superstition should be so rampant in our times. Yet this is happening in a world which proclaims proudly that it is on the verge of an atomic age whose explorers, especially in the fields of atomic physics and biology, rush on from one triumph to the next; a world which is preparing to enter the vast regions of space, which is on the track of a *world formula* which will help to fathom all the movements and changes of matter.

Thirty years ago, a penetrating observer, Count Ernst von Reventlow, foretold the dawn of an *age of magic*, because the longer men took a purely materialistic view of the world, the less it satisfied them. Indeed the conception of the world given by scientific research, which examines the varied abundance of nature and life in laboratories and reduces it to formulae, shows a dangerous one-sidedness. It is crystal clear but it lacks mystery. It makes a show of laws and formulae whose figures operate in a world of bloodless abstractions far removed from real life. It analyses processes and objects down to the last detail, but is unable to convince us that this comprises and explains everything. Behind every problem solved loom new ones which confront the

5

searching mind with obscurities of which it had no inkling hitherto.

For this reason few people expect from scientific research a final answer to the question of the nature and existence of life. Where then can such an answer be found?

Here the ways part. Some turn to Holy Scripture. Here is to be found God's revelation, timeless, valid, profoundly deep, ever revealing to faith new dimensions of God's truth. Others follow the reasonings of magical and superstitious thought in an attempt to fathom the hidden realities of the world. For this they have the help of a rich millennial tradition. Modern superstition is not a modern creation. It is only a revivification of old ideas. New only are the trappings and vocabulary, the theoretical proofs and the examples given. The core is age-old.

Equally old is the conflict between faith and superstition. Faith is the devoted service of the creature to his Creator. It is lived out in trust, obedience and love. In superstition, the deep-rooted will of man seeks to seize hold of the divine and make the powers of the invisible world serve his own needs and desires. It offers directions and methods for getting these powers into our clutches so that we may control and use them. The superstitious man is not therefore *primitive* or a survival from the past. He is separated from the Christian believer by a wide abyss, even when he is parading ideas and sayings from the Bible.

To confront superstition with faith is a highly important task for our times. It is not merely a matter of the contradictions between two theories or world philosophies. Nor is it sufficient to offer exposures and cheap jibes in argument. The roots of superstition have struck deep and they will not be eradicated if one only tries to deal with symptoms. The roots will only lose their vigour when we have succeeded in breaking through into the freedom of the children of God. That requires a total revolution.

Dr. Bauer's book gives valuable help for this purpose. It has grown out of many years' preoccupation with the various fields of superstition. It gives knowledge that has been ripened by rich experience. It does not trail off into condescension or sweeping judgments of a superficial nature such as you find so often with hardboiled rationalists. It extracts by critical examination the elements of truth which are utilised in the cosmic conceptions of superstition while drawing at the same time a sharp distinction between superstition and faith. So the book gives true enlightenment and guidance and in the final chapter offers important advice on pastoral work. May it help the faithful to examine themselves and the superstitious to find freedom!

KURT HUTTEN

Contents

Sources of Diagrams

p. 21   Number symbolism; from *Christus und die Caesaren* (Ethelbert Stauffer), Hamburg 1948

p. 57   Diagram 5; from *Zeitschrift für Parapsychologie*, Bern

p. 129   Diagram 8; from *Handbuch über das Weltall* (Meyer), Mannheim

pp. 133–4   Diagrams 9–10; from *Steht es in den Sternen?* (Ludwig Reiner), Munich 1951

1

The Nature and Basis
of Superstition

Its Nature

MODERN man is faced with a triple choice between unbelief, belief
or superstition.

By unbelief is meant a purely materialistic outlook on the
world, what Paul Tillich calls "a self-contained finitude". Its
adherents know only of this world and believe only what can be
seen, explained, formulated and proved.

The believer, on the other hand, feels that this world is funda-
mentally a riddle and incomplete. He counts on there being an
eternity behind and beyond this finitude. The purpose of life is
not contained within the span of birth and death, nor within
world history with all its ups and downs, its growth and decay,
its struggles and sufferings, its sorrows and sin. He thinks in terms
of Heb. 13:14. "For here we have no continuing city, but we seek
one to come."

Millions make the first choice and millions more make the second though many individuals frequently vacillate between the two.
Those who adopt the third alternative are also counted by the
million and if current trends are to be believed, their number is
on the increase.

A whole army of fortune-tellers and clairvoyants are giving
people advice on their problems. There are said to be ten
thousand in Berlin alone. Most periodicals and illustrated
weeklies publish horoscopes, and an enormous number of astrological calendars are on sale everywhere. Diviners with rod
and pendulum investigate the mysterious rays that emanate
from the soil and attribute such a dreaded disease as cancer
to their influence.

Amulets and talismans for warding off misfortune are manufac-
tured in great quantities; quacks extol their wonder drugs which
they have obtained from abroad; exorcists offer powerful protection against witches and evil spirits; stories of ghosts and devil-

possession are often retailed; spiritualists claim to communicate with the spirits of the dead.

The Demoscopic Institute at Allenbach reports that twenty per cent of the population of West Germany claim to have had some occult experience. The well-known pastor and psychologist, Kurt E. Koch, estimates that eighty per cent of the people who come to his meetings are influenced by psychic powers.

As in every other sphere of modern life, big business has taken advantage of this fashion. One firm which makes an instrument for protecting people from earth rays, sold £70,000 worth in one year. Large publishing firms are engaged exclusively in printing pamphlets and other writings on occultism. These publications have been strongly condemned by the Jesuit Father, Philipp Schmidt, who is an authority on the subject. "This literature contains nothing scientific whatsoever. One has only to look at the advertisements in many of the newspapers and periodicals to see how shamefully their readers are being taken in. The literature of occultism and superstition is mostly a specialised form of smut and trash ... It is no exaggeration to say that sex is the central theme in most of the books of this kind; that is what makes them so saleable."

It is impossible to say how much spiritual harm is being done to simple-minded or credulous people or how much money is being extracted from them. Even so-called educated people are often taken in. Nor is this surprising. The famous Swiss psychoanalyst, C. G. Jung, has shown that rationalism and superstition are complementary; that is to say the one completes the other. The more people devote their lives to a purely rationalistic purpose the less are they able to stand up to life's emotional crises. They then look round for something stronger to hold on to. Having starved their spiritual faculties, they have neither the courage to revive their belief in the supreme Being nor the patience to submit to their fate. So they grasp at the lesser-demanding solution of superstition. A fortune-teller is asked to drive away fear and a piece of chain obtained for protection.

A typical example of this was given in a television broadcast commemorating the loss of the *Titanic* fifty years ago. In 1912 this proud ship was ripped open by an iceberg and sank with 1,500 people on board.

In the broadcast two survivors, a man and a woman, told how they were saved.

The man, who was quite young at the time, had happened to come on deck and quickly realised that his life was in danger. He warned his friends and the people in the next cabin, fetched his overcoat and lifebelt, took a bottle of whisky and a couple of sandwiches from the buffet counter and hurried to the nearest boat which was just being lowered.

The woman, who was a child at the time, had woken up in fright. She first seized her favourite toy, a cloth pig her mother had given her, and then, amid the general panic, had managed to get near one of the boats. She would never have reached it but for a sailor who, in the best tradition, wanted to save the women and children first. In the dark he thought the stuffed pig was a baby. He snatched it from what he took to be its mother's arms and handed it down into the boat. In despair at losing her talis- man, the child pushed her way to the side of the ship and made a daring leap into the same boat.

In the course of the broadcast she held up the pig with great delight and called it her "life saver". It is still her most precious possession.

Anyone can find this typically superstitious strain either in himself or in some of his acquaintances. Many good Christians, and even some pastors, fail to penetrate to it in others because they never become intimate enough with them. Theologically-minded persons maintain a studious reserve and do not take such things seriously. Yet it is this partiality for the occult that keeps many people away from church and, of course, from taking any responsibility for their community, because superstition always isolates a man and makes him concentrate on himself. In addition to the blatant propaganda of the occult sects there is the equally dangerous and harmful decline in faith due to this self-centredness which superstition engenders.

What then is the nature of this vague and widespread superstition (in German *Aberglaube*)? The derivation of the word does not help much. It means a contrary, erroneous or opposite belief. In so far as it is a belief it is therefore of some value.

From the point of view of positivist philosophy, which confines itself to what can be experienced or proved, anything that goes beyond this tested experience is mere superstition; so are a great many of the so-called popular beliefs in the eyes of those who are more advanced culturally or who follow higher forms of religion. It is difficult therefore to draw a dividing line that can be universally applied. The following three considerations appear to be fundamental to it.

1. By belief in its widest sense we mean devotion to a higher, supernatural Power and the submission to it of one's life and desire for happiness. As Martin Luther put it: "We are to fear God above all else, to love Him and put our trust in Him."

The superstitious man, however, seeks to gain control over this Power. By his knowledge or the practice of certain rites he outwits both fate and future and becomes lord of his own life. Superstition always shows a lack of fear of God and trust in Him.

2. Belief involves integration in society and consequently, where the well-being of one's fellows demands it, renunciation and sacrifice. "Thou shalt love thy neighbour as thyself."

The superstitious man seeks his own happiness and security first. He is solely out to satisfy his instincts and desires. The powers and practice of magic enable him to do so. You can read in handbooks of astrology such questions as "How can I win a lottery quickly?" or "Which women can be seduced?" Or they give instructions how to stick a pin into the eyes of a person's photograph in order to do him harm. Fear, greed, lust for happiness are often so strong that all social and moral ties, all rational considerations are swept aside.

3. Usually there is a third consideration related to the other two. It concerns the relationship of superstition to scientific research and cosmology. True belief and true science can never be in conflict, for each knows its own limits. God and the divine cannot be the subject of science otherwise they would be part of the discoverable universe, which is science's domain. The God we know by faith cannot be proved by science. However far the space traveller goes in the universe he will never find God in bodily form.

Belief has purely personal significance. It recognises, of course, the laws of nature and their interrelations but at the same time it ranges them under a higher order of things not perceptible to the senses or, as the Bible might have put it, under the merciful rule of God the Father Almighty.

If, for example, a soldier escapes wounding from a hail of shrapnel, experts in physics and ballistics might explain that the bullets didn't hit him for quite natural reasons. If the man himself doesn't believe in God he will say "I was lucky." If he believes in God he will gratefully recognise that God has saved him.

This is a different attitude from the one which trusts to a stuffed pig. The pig may indeed be the starting point, but not the real cause of an escape. It could well be shown to fail in other cases. How many people have already perished with their talismans, as witness the famous racing motorist, Bernd Rosemeyer, who died in an accident on the Frankfurt-Darmstadt autobahn on his unlucky day, though he was wearing the old red shirt he always wore when racing.

It is typical of the superstitious that they are never convinced by logical proof. They do not want to be enlightened even when rational argument is most in place. They cling on to obscure causes that have long since been disproved by science such as that the moon causes the weather or that foot and mouth disease can be prevented by putting a copper ring under the cowshed floor.

Superstition always denotes a break with science. While the true scientist will leave the supra-rational and inscrutable alone, and even respect them, he will never accept as true what is contrary to reason.

The Roots of Superstition

Why is superstition so widespread today? It has become a disease of our whole civilisation. Why is the engineer in an atom factory as superstitious as the Indian in the Gran Chaco who is untouched by our civilisation? One reason which has been mentioned already is the *complementary relationship between pure rationalism and primitive superstition*. Another is the pendulum of history which, after two hundred years of rationalism is swinging back to the irrational. The puzzling nature of human history and man's whole existence on earth is turning men's minds from rational proof to irrational supposition.

The fact that many superstitious ideas are not pure nonsense gives them substance and leads to their persistence. They contain a grain of truth derived perhaps from some obscure piece of knowledge from ancient times or from some real event which, because of its puzzling nature, gave rise to a false interpretation. We must beware of throwing away the baby with the bath water. Not everything which does not fit into the pattern of modern science can be called superstitious nonsense.

There is a science of superstition which believes in the scientific method and claims to be able to explain and solve every problem in spite of the contention of the famous physicist, Werner Heisenberg, that "all our knowledge hovers over an abyss of ignorance". Over against the "hypnosis experts", as those who explored and supported supra-sensitive perception were called, stand the non-believers who will not recognise anything abnormal or supernatural.

Side by side with the occultism that is based on a confusion of preconceived ideas and prejudices, is one which shows genuine psychic phenomena. Just as chemists once had to struggle to free themselves from many of the absurd ideas of the alchemists in order to be able to observe nature accurately, and just as today we are rediscovering here and there some truth in the content of alchemy, so the same thing is happening with the scientific research into psychic phenomena such as telepathy, clairvoyance, spiritualism, spiritual healing, the magnetic powers of the water diviner, and so on.

Anyone wishing to combat superstition must undertake the task of sifting out truth from falsehood, reality from deception and what can be proved from what can be disproved in these various fields and must examine their limitations.

In the last twenty or thirty years this branch of research has come to be known as parapsychology. The term is not well chosen. The Greek prefix *para* means "beside" or "beyond", whereas parapsychology is really ordinary psychology applied to the frontiers of the spiritual world. The word occult is also misleading. All scientific research is concerned with uncovering what lies hidden and clarifying what is obscure. This is the course we shall adopt in the following chapters. In doing so we shall see how again and again, because of the very nature of these occult and paranormal phenomena, superstition intervenes to confuse truth with falsehood and so cause a great deal of harm.

Today we are in a better position to go into these matters than were the psychologists of the nineteenth century who pinned their faith to science only. When C. G. Carus discovered the subconscious (*Psyche* 1846) our knowledge of the nature of man took a great step forward. The title of Alexis Carrel's book *Man the Unknown* may still be true, but men like Freud, Adler and Jung among others have penetrated far into the depths of man's inner life.

Above all it was recognised that the principle *cogito ergo sum* ("I think therefore I am") enunciated by Descartes, the founder of rationalism, had led men on a false path with serious consequences. The view spread imperceptibly that intelligence was the real nature of man and that therefore he was a purely rational being.

However much the various schools of thought in depth psychology may disagree, there is now a consensus of opinion that man is not this rational, integrated personality. Under the thin layer of consciously and rationally conditioned processes there is a surge of passions, complexes, instincts, distortions and resistances. It is almost as if the real ego were in constant conflict with a blind, greedy, almost bestial driving force and can only rarely carry out the ideal visions of the super-ego (what Jung calls the "self"), which works from above.

Freud has made a brilliant discovery which will help our enquiry into the power and extent of superstition. He describes every instinctive urge as an atavism, i.e. as the aftermath of a former state and the longing to return to it.

This former state may represent an earlier stage in the life of every child and enable us to probe into the urges and phobias of prenatal life. It may also give a clue to the personality of man from earliest times. This personality with all its primal instincts and conflicts, may be living on still in our subconscious mind. Part of our nature still remains primitive and age-old instincts come to life again, even in the modern rationalist who may wish to deny it.

Primitive man's picture of the world was shot through and through with magic, as we know. It is so deeply rooted in us that it is difficult to eradicate. It is always pushing up to the surface, like weeds, especially at a time like the present when so many people are losing their faith.

Many genuine occult experiences derive their power from our unconscious psyche. That is why they often bewilder modern man who only knows the world of his conscious mind, which is governed by natural laws which he can calculate and understand. Until C. G. Jung explored the vast range of powers and possibilities at the deep levels of the subconscious we had no idea of their existence. But we are inseparably bound up with the collective unconscious life of the human race and the original, world-wide concepts of magic. It is these old concepts which come surging up in our dreams and occult experiences.

2

Belief in the Magic Power of Charms and Spells

Magic and Life

IN speaking of primitive man I do not use the term in any derogatory sense. It would perhaps be better to speak of prehistoric man, for that gives a fundamental difference between him and ourselves. He lacked our awareness of the continuous march of events in an irrevocable form. It would certainly be a great mistake to describe prehistoric man, or even men still living in a state of savagery, as superstitious. What appears to modern man as a departure from rational processes may be for prehistoric man merely keeping within the appropriate framewok of *his* emotional life, which, for him, is not the limited period between birth and death, but participation in the life of the tribe and the honourable fulfilment of his role in it.

Death does not mean the same thing to him as it does to us. It is exclusion from the tribe, dishonour, cowardice or some accident which, even if it does not prove fatal, amounts in his eyes to death. A weakling baby can be abandoned if it has not yet been owned by the father, without the flicker of an eyelid; a prisoner of war may be slain because, by his very misfortune he is dead already. In the same way a widow can only live on by being buried with her husband or by committing suicide. Our ideas of life and death, the customs we have derived from Christianity and history are completely inapplicable here. Man lives not for himself alone; he only lives as part of the family or tribe. Masks, magic and even some of the cruel rituals that seem to us so revolting, are means to protect, strengthen and purify life. Therefore magic makes sense to these people. Their whole existence is enfolded in a *unio magica* (magical union).

We have therefore no grounds for looking down on primitive man; rather there are good reasons for warning modern man against trying to return to a world which is quite different and quite foreign to him, one which he would soon reject because it does not fit in either with *his* nature, *his* conscience or *his* judgment.

There is a further fundamental difference between primitive man and the superstitious man who suddenly reverts to the primitive man's world. The former was completely at home in it and was prepared to sacrifice for it and even to obey its ruthless customary laws. The latter, on the other hand, makes use of magic to secure his own selfish happiness. He is by no means prepared to sacrifice or put himself aside. The more he gets involved in magical practices like exorcism and spellbinding, the lower his moral standards fall.

Let us take some examples of this reversion to a belief in magic. Our first ancestors did not think in the same terms of cause and effect which we have accepted as true. They thought more in terms of *analogy* and correspondences. They thought that things went on as they always had been at the beginning— as in heaven so on earth. This idea is met with again in the writings of the astrologers.

Thinking in analogies can often be met with today. If a bridegroom happens to stumble when he is leading his bride up the steps to the altar, some aunt or cousin is bound to whisper: It will be his fault if the marriage goes wrong. Or if a huntsman meets a feeble old woman as he is leaving his hunting box in the morning, he will curse his luck and not go hunting because he believes that the age and weakness of the woman will affect his shooting. Motorists foresee an accident if they happen to get out of bed on the left side. Primitive man always thought the right side better, partly because that is the side on which the sun rises when he is facing the home of his ancestors in the North.

Of course the rule: As it was in the beginning is now and ever shall be, will often find confirmation today. H. Benger has pointed out that there is in man a fatalistic urge to disaster which leads him to concoct accidents in his disturbed imagination merely out of fear. A nervous cyclist will be drawn *as if by magic* to the one large stone in the road which causes him to fall off. We see here, as we shall see later on, what a great power fear exercises over us.

The belief in *Mana* is another deeply-rooted idea of the past. It is met with in the South Sea Islands in the Pacific Ocean. It represents a mysterious essence which make those who possess it strong and victorious, whether it be a chief or the whole tribe. When a powerful enemy has been killed and his flesh and blood been *incorporated* in the eater, the latter acquires the strength of his victim. This is the explanation of cannibalism. It is not a question of hunger.

Reverence for the dead may also spring from this idea. By careful preservation of the body of an ancestor you store up a kind of reservoir of strength.

Mana may be found not only in living things but also in inanimate objects such as stones of a peculiar shape or colour, jewels, a leopard's claw or a wolf's tooth. If a Polynesian has a barren breadfruit tree, he goes in search of stones that look a bit like a breadfruit and buries them in the earth round his tree. In this case *mana* is being used for imitative magic.

Carrying objects endowed with such power on one's person gives protection against evil spirits, hence the belief in amulets and the confidence placed in talismans and fetishes. We can see in this the strong link which connects Stone Age man with his modern counterpart. Skiers wear a medallion portraying Saint Ulrich as a protection against falls. Society women select a jewel for their ring which will bring them luck and good health. Motorists hang mascots in their car to ward off accidents. Famous footballers rely on teddy-bears to help them shoot more goals. As we have already seen, Bernd Rosemeyer swore by his faded red shirt. Thousands of people wear small horseshoes or clover leaves. This may only be a fashion now, but at the back of their minds lurks the subconscious thought: *There may be something in it.*

Protective magic is sometimes met with in the arts. Ugly, grinning faces have been carved outside many romanesque and gothic churches with the purpose of driving away evil spirits. Shrovetide customs too have their origin in magic. People thought they could drive winter away by wearing hideous masks, yelling and engaging in vigorous dances. They believed that in this way they were clearing the path for spring. Folklore and folk customs are intimately bound up with these ideas.

Sacred Numbers and Letters

In olden times numbers and letters were regarded with the same reverence as the horseshoe which was revered partly because iron was scarce and partly because the horse was such a valuable animal. It may also have been because the shoe was shaped like the crescent of the moon. Numbers and letters were then used as a means of controlling nature and were thought to possesses the same power as *mana*.

Modern man working at his bench or sitting in his office attaches no special significance to numbers. One figure is as good as another. Even so, he often succumbs to a superstitious fear which makes him believe in lucky and unlucky numbers.

On closer examination this belief in special numbers, like the traditions of astrology, does not derive from a common origin. The experience of one tribe led them to regard a number as sacred that another tribe thought to be harmful. Thus many American tribes, from Eskimoes in the north to Tierrafuegans in the south regard four, not three, as having sacred significance.

In early Christian times, the Jews regarded thirteen as definitely lucky. In our western culture, from the time of Pythagoras in the sixth century B.C., odd numbers have been considered to be more luck-bringing than even ones. This was due to the impingement on western thought of oriental asceticism which attributed masculine virility to odd numbers and feminine weakness to even numbers, so the latter became tainted with what was shameful and sensual.

How then did thirteen come to be thought unlucky? Numerous attempts have been made to explain it. Many tribes worshipped the moon and believed it was a woman. Hence the name for moon in most languages is feminine. Both Jews and Arabs divide their year into thirteen moons or months. When, however, men began to worship the sun, they divided their year into twelve months. To make both years coincide, a thirteenth month had often to be inserted, and this upset the harmony of calculation. So the number thirteen came to be regarded as old-fashioned, superfluous and even harmful. Moreover many of those who clung to the old faith suffered misfortune. There is also the story of Judas, the thirteenth at table, who betrayed his Master.

People who are afraid of this number easily get entangled in a chain reaction of auto-suggestions which bring about the thing they fear. I heard of an acquaintance who arrived late for dinner and suddenly became aware that he was the thirteenth guest. That same evening he fell ill, not because he was the thirteenth guest but because of his superstitious credulity.

The idea of ill-luck attaching to Friday is another example. Many Germanic tribes worshipped Freya, the goddess of love, matrimony and the home. The horse was her sacred animal. One was sacrificed on Friday the feast day, and many were killed and eaten at weddings. For this reason, the Church forbade weddings on Fridays and the eating of horse-flesh, lest any Christians should revert to their heathen beliefs. This explains why many people refuse to eat meat on Fridays or start on any undertaking. Black cats were also sacred to Freya and were said to bring bad luck.

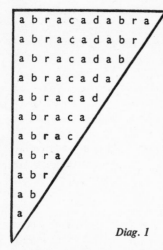

a b r a c a d a b r a
a b r a c a d a b r
a b r a c a d a b
a b r a c a d a
a b r a c a d
a b r a c a
a b r a c
a b r a
a b r
a b
a

Diag. 1

Then came the crucifixion of Christ on a Friday. But here we see the superficial nature of the superstition, which fails to grasp the more serious import of that day. For the Christian it is not only a day of mourning for sin, but a day of liberation; not a day that brings bad luck, but one that brings salvation. That is why Martin Luther called it *Good* Friday.

Like certain numbers, letters have long been regarded with mysterious awe. Originally they were made out of sticks of beech wood which were used for magic signs and to cast lots. They were thrown on the ground and gathered up in an order which was supposed to tell whether an action would bring success or failure.

Strange words thought to have magical power, like the Egyptian abracadabra, have long been known. This word was set out in diminishing form (Diagram 1). As each form was read out sickness and disease were expected likewise to diminish. It was much used in the Middle Ages and by the Romans whom Tacitus cursed for liking such loathsome things.

A similar use was made of the famous *sator* formula (Diagram 2). The letters form a magic quadrilateral. The letters can be read from left to right, right to left, top to bottom or bottom to top. It was used to ward off sickness, storms, witchcraft or fire.

In Saxony in 1742, an official regulation was laid down which said: "We hereby give it to be known to all our subordinates that great poverty can result from damage by fire. Such disasters must therefore be controlled in time. We therefore order that a supply of wooden plates on the accompanying model be kept in every town and village, so that when a fire breaks out, they can be thrown on to it in the name of God and put it out." The rationalists of the time might well be pardoned for going to extremes in rejecting both superstition and faith when they read such a document.

This *sator* formula was known to the people of Pompeii. A copy was found in one of their houses. The formula has also been given a Christian significance. The letters can be arranged in the form

Diag. 2

S	A	T	O	R
A	R	E	P	O
T	E	N	E	T
O	P	E	R	A
R	O	T	A	S

Diag. 3

of a cross (Diagram 3). They then make the word Paternoster vertically and horiontally, ending with an A and O which recalls the alpha and omega of the Book of Revelation.

Sacred signs and numbers were used by the early Church, as well as being found in the Bible. The sign of the fish appears frequently in the catacombs of Rome and Syracuse. Peter was known as the great fisherman and the baptismal font was called a piscina, meaning a fish pond. What is most remarkable is that the letters of the Greek word for fish give the Greek initials for Jesus Christ, Son of God, Saviour.

```
        A
        .
        P
        A
        T
        E
A·PATERNOSTER·O
        O
        S
        T
        E
        R
        .
        O
```

Number symbolism certainly plays an important part in the Bible, as it does in the Jewish cabala of later times. For example Matthew's Gospel is ingeniously based on the numbers 3 and 7. Many numbers of special significance are also found in the Book of Revelation. In chapter 13, verse 18 it says: "Here is wisdom. Let him that hath understanding count the number of the beast, for it is the number of a man and his number is 666."

Antiquity knows of many such numerical riddles, for letters were indicated by numbers. Scratched on a wall in Pompeii is a declaration which reads: "I love her whose number is 545." Clearly there could be many explanations of such riddles. Dr.

A–utokrator	=	1
Kai–sar=20+1+10	=	31
Domet–ianos=4+70+40 } + 5+300 }	=	419
Seb–astos= 200+ 5+ 2	=	207
Ge–rmanicos=3+ 5	=	8
		——
		666
		——

The letters before the hyphen are those found on the coin.

Deissmann interpreted the number 666 as meaning "The Emperor is God"; but it really stands for a person's name, either the tyrant emperor Caligula or the equally tyrannical emperor Nero. Strangely enough the numerical value of the abbreviations of the official title of the emperor stamped on a coin of Domitian also add up to 666.

Among the Babylonians the figure 12 was a symbol of harmony and abundance. In the Bible it also indicates completion. On the other hand the 4 of the points of the compass represents the omnipresence of God.

As regards numbers in general we may adopt Jakob Böhme's and Friedrich Christoph Oetinger's interpretation of 1 as being used to designate the Creator. The figure 2 means separation from God and the resultant despair. Three was the re-unification through God's spirit in the Trinity. Four is separation raised to a higher power, the remoteness of God. So the forty years in the wilderness and Jesus' forty days and nights of fasting. Seven is the re-union of the Trinity with separation, which thus becomes the completion of salvation. Ten or twelve represents abundance. Many other things could be explained and connections drawn in this way.

There is of course a very real danger of playing tricks with numbers. Biblical number symbolism furthermore cannot be reduced to a common denominator or fitted into a closed system. There is plenty of scope for arbitrary judgment, personal interpretation and dealing in mysteries. Thousands of connections more or less appropriate are to be found in the realm of numbers. Here as elsewhere, the Bible makes use of material already fashioned by non-Christian ideas, but it seeks to construct a very different edifice from a heathen temple. Many pagan religions regard the world as a cosmos, a harmony governed by law and order. The Biblical writers know that this harmony has been destroyed by man's sin. Therefore no earthly law, no playing with numbers can ever be a true revelation of God's plan and counsel. Three and four may make seven but they do not possess the compelling power that can bring about, in the reality of history, anything approaching the complete salvation of man. God's grace is always His free gift.

That is why taking the number 666 so seriously was really a departure from the main point. If we allow these numerical puzzles to whet our curiosity too much, we shall miss the real theme of the Book of Revelation, which was to comfort and strengthen the Christian community at a time of persecution. This is where many sects go astray. Instead of grasping the main point,

they get bogged down in things of secondary importance. That
is satanic.

We must, however, be clear on one fundamental point as regards sacred amulets, letters and numbers. Since the coming of
Christ there have no longer been any *sacred* objects in the strict
sense of the word. By totally rejecting the Pharisees' rules on
purity (Mark 7: 14 ff.), Jesus abolished all distinctions between
clean and unclean, between sacred and profane. There is no
sphere of human life that is not of this earthly world but there
is equally none which cannot be sanctified by grateful enjoyment
or obedient service to God. To single out any earthly object and
attribute to it special sanctity or virtue always means setting up
a power in opposition to God the Creator. In other words, belief
in amulets or lucky and unlucky numbers is idolatry of such
a primitive kind that intelligent men should have left it behind
long ago. If we know ourselves to be in the care of a kind but
invisible God, why should we cling on to earthly idols which are
transient and powerless? The reason lies deeper than mere human
weakness or innocence. Too many men today have almost entirely lost faith and trust in the wisdom and guidance of a God
who holds and sustains our life in His hands.

Let Christians show then that they have no fear of Fridays or
thirteens. If anyone enquires after our health, let us cheerfully
acknowledge that we are very well, thank you, without adding
some such anxious remark as, "touch wood". We should not fear
the power of evil spirits or demons. It is God alone who gives
and takes away health. Above all objects sanctified by man, let
us endeavour to glorify Him and live in personal touch with Him
through Christ, for He says: "Be ye holy, even as I am holy"
(Leviticus 19: 2).

Sorcery and Books of Spells

A particularly confused picture is presented by books of magic
which seek to secure happiness, wealth, healing and sexual indulg-
ence by the use of magic wands and incantations.

The sixteenth-century book of spells, Fausti Höllenzwang, is
well known. A popular book current in Germany is one called
the *Sixth and Seventh Books of Moses*. It purports to give the
"secret of all secrets and Moses's dealings with familiar spirits,
faithfully copied from the original manuscript." It was first published somewhere between 1520 and 1540 and contains the usual
re-hash of Egyptian, cabalistic and Arab prayers and formulae for
exorcism, some of them blasphemous in nature. The book reveals

the complete selfishness, crass folly and immorality of those who practise such things. In 1956 a magistrates' court in Brunswick fined the publishers heavily and confiscated their plant and presses together with all the copies of the book. For some incomprehensible reason this decision was reversed by the court of appeal and the book is now enjoying a wider circulation than ever!

In the sixth book, the Triune God and Lucifer, the prince and ruler of darkness, are called upon in one and the same breath, and instructions are given for making a pact with the devil. Then follow incantations in the names of Adoni, Eloim, Ariel and Jehovah, which enable you to find treasure, converse with the dead or foresee the future in a crystal (Solomon's mirror). They will also help you by the aid of spirits to wreak vengeance on an enemy.

The seventh book bears the title *A Treasury of Sympathetic Magic for the Attainment, by Well-tried Means, of Various Ends.* The publishers recommend, somewhat hypocritically, that in cases of sickness a doctor should be called. One or two examples will serve to show what nonsense it all is.

Protection against Witches: Put on odd shoes; wear your shirt or a stocking inside out. Wear a bunch of four-leaved clover. Hang a "disturber" from the ceiling made up of the bones from a carp's head arranged in the form of a dove, or a whole empty shell provided with paper wings and a head. The continual swinging of this disturber will drive away witches.

How to Harm People: If you want to harm an enemy, take a sheet of glass. Write on it in ink and after sunset, the following words: Misfortune will come upon you; your wickedness be on your own head, N.N.! Then wash the glass plate with dirty water and pour this out at your enemy's doorstep. If you wish utterly to destroy him, break or bury the glass in front of his house.

A Magic Charm against all Sickness: If a man is dangerously ill, take some of his urine, boil a piece of pork in it till it is nearly done and give it to a stray dog to eat. The patient will get better and the dog will die.

For Weak Eyesight: Hang the eyes of a toad at the back of the neck. This will preserve your features, strengthen your eyes and ward off every other frailty.

These magic prescriptions and spells are as widespread as they are foolish. They are the source of much envy and hate, and serve to spread disease. The cure for syphilis is to have yourself buried up to the neck in fresh horse manure!

To conclude, it must once more be made clear that all this conjuring of spirits and use of spells offends against the first commandment. Men are here attempting to force God and fate to do what they want instead of using their commonsense and praying humbly for God's help, no matter whether He grants it or not.

A distinction is often made between Black and White magic, as though they were different. Surely, if we demand physical healing (without any willingness for God's plan in our lives), but make use of the names of God in our prayer, which is White Magic, we are just as wrong as those who use spells, or call upon the Devil, to obtain the ends that they wish for. It is rebellion against the kindness and goodness of God, the original sin. In every form of superstition there is a danger of being separated from God and becoming the slave of powers that work against Him.

Use and Abuse in Churches

For the Protestant who lives in a community with differing faiths, the question naturally arises: What about many of the practices of the Roman Catholic Church? What happens when candles, bells or medallions are *blessed*? What about sacred relics? Is the Catholic Mass only valid when it is celebrated on an altar or a portable altar containing the relics of some saint or martyr?

In my view, words like superstition, swindle or duping of the masses are out of place in any serious discussion. The condemnations of Martin Luther, who talked of the devil's mart and spared neither scorn nor ridicule, sprang from the large number of abuses that characterised the Chuch of his day. In 1505, Duke Frederick the Wise exhibited 5,000 relics in his private chapel in Wittenberg.

In the canon law of the Roman Catholic Church, the paragraph dealing with these matters has been very carefully drawn up by such experts in dogmatic theology as Bartmann and Schmaus. It expresses considerable caution in attaching particular value to the objects used to represent the sacraments. The emphasis is not laid on the symbols but on the prayers and the spiritual effect. These theologians also expressly warn against reliance on holiness coming automatically through material means. They call that superstition. *The Catholic hopes for the spiritual blessing, not directly from any special object he may wear, such as a medallion, but from a devout attitude of complete trust in the goodness of God and of submission to His will.* It is further emphasised that the Catholic Church reaches the simple-minded through what pleases the senses and that the grace of God should affect even bodily needs.

In spite of this, the Protestant has grounds for serious doubt. Do Catholics really mean what they say when they assert that God alone is holy and that holiness resides in no earthly thing? Is God's grace really understood as His personal love for us and not as some force we make use of? Do they not come very near to meeting popular beliefs and superstition, especially in countries like Italy and Spain? Will not simple-minded men be led by all these blessings and dedications to think of Christianity as a bringer of good luck, i.e. to the view that God is there only to see that all goes well with them and to fulfil their earthly desires?

How welcome it would be if the procession following the coffin of the three Holy Kings in Cologne was centred on Christ instead of the three saints, as many Catholic priests would like! How good it would be if sprinkling with holy water ceased to be a formality or a magic source of protection and was connected in the believer's mind with the prayers the Church offers for him! Surely there is a danger of misuse. That is why, following Calvin's example, Protestant churches have rightly abolished these customs. It is easy to forget what Protestants call the second commandment: "Thou shalt not make unto thyself any graven image nor likeness." This means that no absolute value must be attached to anything material and that we should be on our guard against trusting in any talisman, idol or occult power.

There are many current abuses in the Protestant church to show that we need to take the beam out of our own eye. I know a sacristan who, instead of throwing away water used for baptism, sold it for between two and five marks. It was said to cure toothache and other ailments. That may be an exception but unfortunately there are many people who use the Bible as a fetish. Goethe made fun of people who shut their eyes and stuck their thumbs into a page hoping to find some special guidance where their thumb pointed. The Bible is not a book for finding oracles. It must be read and studied (Acts 17: 11) and the purpose of this study is not to find clues to the future but union with Christ, our Lord.

3

Telepathy, Clairvoyance and Soothsaying

SPELLBINDING, sorcery and conjuring up spirits take us far back in time. They belong to primitive man's conception of his world and show what, for contemporary man, has become superstition. But is it possible to say the same of occult phenomena which a large number of scientists today take for fact? Are telepathy, clairvoyance and soothsaying a swindle or just imagination, or are we dealing here with phenomena that have been insufficiently studied and not yet explained?

Examples

These three procedures have often been regarded as the same thing but they should be kept separate.

By telepathy is meant the supra-sensitive perception of another person's conscious state. It is not the same as thought-reading so called. It is being sensitive to states of mind in others connected with some emotion; to another person's desires, fears, hopes, motives and feelings. By supra-sensitive I mean unconnected with normal observation, empathy or logical processes and combinations of thought.

For example, a noted woman fortune-teller in Paris was consulted by the mother of a seventeen-year-old boy who was suffering from a disease of the hip joint. There was a fear that he might contract consumption of the lung. Without knowing anything of this, the fortune-teller succeeded in stating, after some consideration, that, according to the cards, the mother had an anaemic son who would die in his twentieth year. Things turned out otherwise. The dreaded year came and went and thereafter the young man improved visibly in health.

This could be explained by saying that the clairvoyante was mistaken. But granted that there is such a thing as telepathy, the

27

explanation is that while reading her cards, the fortune-teller, far from discovering any fact entirely unknown to the mother and the boy, had tapped through telepathy, the subconscious fears of the mother and had interpreted them as a fact.

Clairvoyance proper must deal with facts that cannot be known to the clairvoyant by any natural means. It is the direct result of non-sensual perception. Advocates of clairvoyance maintain that the factor of distance plays no part. The clairvoyant sees far distant events and can recount what he sees.

The most notable example of this is the vision that the famous Swedish pastor and philosopher, Emanuel Swedenborg, had in 1759. Reliable witnesses confirm it in the following report.

Swedenborg was returning from England and had landed in Gothenberg. He was sitting at lunch with several leading citizens. Suddenly he became very disturbed and began telling them he could see Stockholm in flames. He even described certain houses and areas that were burning. Several days later a courier arrived from Stockholm, a distance of 300 kilometres, and brought news of a conflagration that had destroyed part of the town. Immanuel Kant, a very critical philosopher, heard this story from someone who was present. It seemed to him very convincing then, but he later became very sceptical and attacked Swedenborg's philosophical fantasies in a tract entitled *Dreams of a Visionary*.

Professor Scherer, who was a secretary in an embassy in Stockholm, gives a similar and equally striking example. An acquaintance of his, a man who feared God and loved the truth, had told him how, on July 17th, 1762, the day on which the Russian Emperor, Peter the Third, died, he was at a social gathering in Amsterdam. Swedenborg was also there. In the middle of a conversation his face suddenly changed. He appeared to be far away, as if something extraordinary was happening before his eyes. As soon as he had recovered himself they asked him what had happened. He did not want to say at first but on being pressed he said: "At this very moment the Emperor Peter III has died in prison". He then described how it had happened and added: "Gentlemen, you have only to compare this day with the official announcement which will appear in the newspapers". That very day the Czar had been overthrown in a revolt led by his wife and murdered.

If examples which surmount space are impressive, how much more so are those which surmount time. How astonishing it would be if there were genuine *prophecy*, or, as the parapsychologists say, precognition, which showed knowledge of future events for which there is no concrete image available, but which somehow *swim into the ken* of the seer. Both in literature and in contemporary experience many such astonishing examples are actually to be found.

In Faust, Goethe refers to a Michael Nostradamus (Michel de Notre Dame), a French astrologer and doctor who lived in the Middle Ages and whose name is enveloped in mystery. He was probably half Jew and half Spaniard and was personal physician to Charles IX of France. He lived from 1503 to 1566. His brilliant prophecies are written in verses of four lines and are printed in ten groups of a hundred verses each. His prophecy for Henry II of France reads:

> *In tourney strange young lion slays the old.*
> *Scratching out eyes behind their cage of gold,*
> *Of both protagonists 'tis one will die*
> *In pain and agony of his wounded eye.*

Four years later this prophecy was fulfilled. In a tournament the king was wounded in the eye by a young nobleman. The lance had pierced the king's golden vizor and he lay in agony for a month before he died. The prophecy had been printed four years earlier in Lyons. For the rest, these sayings are mostly arranged in such a disorderly way and are so ambiguous that almost anything can be read from them, either about the present or the future.

Johann Kaspar Lavater, the Swiss pastor and writer, who was a friend of Goethe and became famous on account of his writings on anatomy, had a well-attested experience of prevision. Several years before his death he said he would die from a bullet wound. At the time this seemed highly improbable. However, when the French occupied Zürich in 1799, Lavater noticed a fellow-citizen being molested by a Frenchman. He went to his rescue and in the scuffle he was wounded by a shot from the Frenchman's rifle. He died after a long illness and his prophecy was fulfilled.

Goethe also believed in such premonitions, as we know from his autobiography. He describes his inner struggles over breaking free from his love for Friederike in Sesenheim. "Under such pressure I could not go without seeing Friederike again. These were distressful times whose memory no longer remains with me. Tears stood in her eyes as I reached down my hand from my horse in farewell and I felt ill. I rode along the footpath to Drusenheim and there I had a strange presentiment. I saw myself, not with my physical eye but with my mind's eye, coming along the path to meet me and wearing clothes such as I had never possessed, soft grey with gold facings. As soon as I had shaken myself out of the dream there was no one there. The strange thing is that I went to visit Friederike eight years later wearing the dress I had seen in the dream. I had chosen it quite by chance. Whatever may be the significance of these things, that remarkable phantom soothed me at the time of our separation."

It is worthwhile noting that these last two examples have to do with the two strongest human emotions—fear of death and love.

As so many Europeans have a boundless respect for what happens in this way in strange and distant lands, especially with the lamas of Tibet, some brief account will not be out of place here.

The teachings of the Buddha give men greater powers of introspection than those possessed by Europeans who live more on the surface of current events. Many secrets of spiritual training (Yoga) have been preserved and taught in schools of asceticism down the ages. One can well believe the numerous reports of lamas who were capable of raising or lowering the temperature of the body by sheer mental power. In the coldest winters they can spend a whole night out of doors in silent meditation without coming to any harm. By slowing down their breathing and pulse they can remain shut up in a confined space for a very long time. This power of controlling the vegetative nervous system is impossible for most Europeans, or perhaps in course of time we have lost the art. But anything that goes beyond this art belongs only to the fertile imagination of the oriental. The European can easily be taken in by it. A few years ago Cyril Henry Hoskins, alias Lobsang Rampa, wrote his famous book *The Third Eye*. It was a best seller and produced a wave of belief in the occult. In reality it was not written by a wise man from the mysterious mountains of Tibet, but by an ordinary English plumber who had never been there! In view of the stir it created, it is not surprising that Kurt Hutten described it as a "wild literary masquerade".

While reverencing these wise men of Tibet or India, one must remember that in Tibet, for example, until recently the poverty was indescribable. Even in the monasteries which sheltered a third of the male population infectious diseases and syphilis raged unchecked and the dirt was beyond words. From this it is evident that true wisdom does not reside in absorption or occult practices, but in mastering life and thinking of one's neighbour. That is the "more excellent way" Paul talks about (1 Cor. 12: 13), a way that goes beyond all magical gifts.

There is no doubt, however, that there has always been genuine clairvoyance among Tibetans. Their whole way of thinking and formal training show this. Yet Heinrich Harrer, who knows them

31

as well as any man, did not gain a favourable impression from his visit to the great national temple.

A young monk in a trance staggers into the circle of dignitaries, wearing a heavy headdress. His face is puffy and smeared with an unhealthy looking red colour. He hisses between his clenched teeth. Suddenly he gives a leap. Servants rush to help him but he escapes them and begins to spin round in a strange, ecstatic dance to the mournful sound of oboes. His groanings and gnashings of teeth are the only human sounds to be heard in the temple. Then one of the ministers begins to ask him questtions which he is supposed to answer. But only half words and indistinct mutterings are heard while an aged secretary records these answers industriously on a tablet. Was he perhaps the real oracle who had once served his turn as the state oracle? asks Harrer. However that may be, all these arts were not able to save the Tibetans from Red occupation and His Divine Majesty, the Dalai Lama, had to flee his country in all haste.

The clever priests of Delphi may also have been the real seers, not the famous python which they stupefied with gases from a crack in the earth.

Returning from distant lands and ancient times, let me quote some examples of clairvoyance or precognition from my own experience.

It was at the beginning of 1941. We knew nothing as yet of Hitler's campaign against Russia. After the victory over France and the Russian treaty, Germany's might seemed firmly established. At this time I got to know a Russian count who was an émigré. One evening I had a clairvoyant session with him in a room lit by one candle. He asked me not to put my question aloud, but only to think it. He would then give the answer. He had a soothsayer's map with about forty different pictures on it and used it to get his subconscious mind working. Putting himself into a kind of trance he laid small bits of paper on some of the pictures and slowly, absent-mindedly, stopping at frequent intervals, spoke something like the following words: "The answer to your question is No! I see a number of small ships approaching a coast. I see an alarm bell (his own word) rising above the ships. I see many planes and thousands of soldiers landing."

After a few moments a second picture came. "I see a broad, brown river with many people drowning in it and it turns blood red."

Finally came a third picture which remains very clear in my memory. "I see many houses in a large town burning and I see many highly-placed people being hanged."

As may be imagined, the question I framed in my own mind was: Will Germany win? The first picture has now become well known. It was the allied landing on June 6th 1944 in Normandy. As regards the third picture, it might easily arise in anyone's mind who had had nightmares about ruins and bombings, but no German in 1941 would have foreseen anything so specific and extraordinary as the hanging of important people. This point can then be regarded as significant, i.e. typical of genuine prevision. There are, however, objections which we shall refer to later on.

The second picture will serve to show that the clairvoyant often doesn't foresee things of general concern and known to everybody but something private to the individual he is with.

In May 1945 I was endeavouring to cross the muddy, swollen waters of the Elbe clinging to the fragment of a bridge that had been blown up. At the same time numbers of soldiers, women and children who had jumped in were drowning. Many were hit by the machine gun fire of the retreating Russians and their blood coloured the water.

Two other cases among my personal friends were concerned with the so-called premonition of death, that is, someone gives a sign to relatives shortly before he dies, often from a great distance and by non-sensual means. Whether signs of recognition or communications have come from the dead or not will be dealt with under the heading of spiritism.

In the year 1943, when I was at home on leave from Russia, I visited the mother of a fallen comrade. She was a simple, trustworthy Christian. She told me that she knew her son was dead a week before the company commander's letter arrived. "I was sitting with my neighbour and we were chatting about things of no great importance when suddenly I was seized with a terrible fear. I saw before me my son in uniform standing in open country. First he stood and then he fell bleeding. I said to my neighbour, 'I know he's dead.' She tried in vain to comfort me."

As so often happens in such cases, the woman was sure that the time of her vision corresponded to the time stated in the commander's letter. On this occasion the son was about 2,000 kilometres away.

The following example, like many others of the same kind, includes an animal among the clairvoyants.

After one of my lectures, two old women came up to me. They were two sisters whom I had known a long time and had found very reliable. They told me the following story. After the last war they had for a time looked after the eight-year-old son of refugees and had become very fond of him. Some time later his parents were in a position to take him back. They were living in a town 300 kilometres away. The boy wrote now and then, but as usually happens, the correspondence finally ceased. Three years later the two sisters were sitting one evening in their room with their faithful Saint Bernard at their feet. Suddenly the dog got up, wagged his tail delightedly and looked towards one corner of the room. The woman followed his gaze and saw the figure of a child in a white nightshirt. He raised his hand and waved sadly to them. Within a few moments the indistinct apparition had disappeared. At first it never occurred to them that this was the shadowy image of their foster son. They remembered him as a much smaller child. They discussed this during the next few days, wondering what it could mean. Then came the sad news that the child had died suddenly from a severe illness.

What strikes you about these three examples is not only the spontaneous and involuntary surprise caused by an apparition. There was also a certain amount of participation. The clairvoyant goes into a trance and the dying persons, clearly concentrating their thoughts on their loved ones, are now able to establish a visual contact in the form of a picture. True it is only an imaginary one, like those formed by the memory, but the recipient projects it outwards, in one case into the corner of the room. This reminds us of the fact well-known to psychologists that children in the stage of puberty and members of primitive tribes are often *eidectic*, which means in part that they are unable to distinguish between the creations of their imagination and the real world outside. They attribute the same reality to both.

Every parapsychologist knows that there are hosts of swindlers and charlatans, but there are also skilful performers who merely want to entertain the public and earn their living. I had the opportunity of making the acquaintance of Mr. E. Hanussen II, the pupil of the famous Hanussen I who was murdered by the Brown Shirts in 1934. The pupil was giving a brilliant performance in the *kursaal* of a North Sea bathing resort. He guessed, for example, the number of a banknote sealed in an envelope. The astonished audience did not see that he was making use of an old trick. He then got five people to write a word on five bits of paper and seal them in different envelopes. He himself used a sixth envelope in which he had placed his own word, e.g. laryngitis. He then held one envelope to his forehead and guessed the contents, using his own word. He opens the envelope in which there is a different word, makes quick note of it and pretends it confirms his guess. Then he guesses the contents of the second envelope, but gives the word of the first which he now knows. He goes on in this way till all the envelopes have been opened and then distributes them haphazard among the crowd who have not noticed the sixth envelope. They believe and are astonished. Of course this requires a considerable amount of skill and memory.

He then uses this successful trick to demand an advance fee of fifteen marks for attendance at his consultation which he holds on the following day. Aided by his knowledge of human nature and a certain charm of manner he makes a number of statements which more or less apply to the case. Naturally his consultations are a great success, especially in the matter of finance!

On the morning after the above performance, as the clairvoyant was about to tell me all sorts of things about my supposed trouble, I interrupted him and asked him to name a large domestic animal I was thinking about. He looked at me suggestively with his blue eyes and said, "That would cost 300 marks". I agreed and felt for my wallet which, incidentally only contained twenty marks. But he declined in alarm. He complained of nervous strain and added that he could not possibly undertake such a task that day. Thereupon I politely took my leave. Possibly I should have told him that the large domestic animal I had in mind was grey and had long ears!

Even genuine clairvoyants cannot keep it up from nine till twelve and two till five in the day. In any case, clairvoyance will occur only at rare moments when the medium is surprised by a mental picture or is visited by a spirit.

Scientific Experiments

As spontaneous experiences of clairvoyance and similar phenomena are rare and often difficult to confirm, people who are interested in the scientific side of them, as well as professional scientists, have endeavoured to produce proof of supra-sensory perception under controlled conditions in a laboratory. I do not wish to speak here of the well-known mediums of the nineteenth and twentieth centuries. Many of them have been exposed as frauds; many became "stars" and from the beginning they were surrounded by people who were all too ready to take their marvels as true. I would rather take first some sober, statistical experiments.

The experiments of J. B. Rhine at Duke University, North Carolina, round about 1930 have become famous, and his book on the extensiveness of the mind (*Die Reichweite des Geistes*) has been widely read. He believes that not only clairvoyants but everybody else has psychic powers and he seeks to prove it by statistics. He took five cards with a simple design on each, a circle, a square, a cross, a star and three wavy lines (Diagram 4).

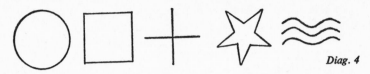

Diag. 4

He then used a pack of these cards consisting of five of each design. The cards are placed face downwards, and as each one is picked up, the person making the experiment has to guess which it is. According to the law of probability, a large number of experiments should produce the result of one correct guess in five, i.e. an average of five in twenty-five. Rudolf Tischner has done some very useful work on this from the parapsychological side. He writes: "With a small series of experiments there is often, of course, the chance of a larger or smaller number of successes on account of *dispersion*. With a larger series the average soon reaches one in five. If in eight games, i.e. 200 guesses, the average is 6.5, the probability is that the result rests on chance, about one in a hundred and fifty, whereas usually the probability of one in a hundred is regarded as a guarantee that the result does not depend on chance. A good average in several hundred guesses is between eight and ten and this cannot be explained by chance.

"Even in a smaller series, the likelihood of chance may recede when a number of correct guesses occur in a row. The probability of nine occurring in a row is one in two million. There were also cases of fifteen in a row (one in thirty million). With twenty-five in a row the probability is one in 298 trillion."

The surprising thing is that students of both sexes, selected at random and most of them intelligent and critical, achieved a much higher average than was to be expected. There were seven, eight, nine and even sixteen to eighteen correct guesses. One student guessed the whole pack right.

Rhine gives precise details of the measures taken to insure scientific control of the experiments. Important results were obtained by making the experiments more difficult. The person doing the experiment was kept at distances ranging from 15 to 900 metres from the cards. In some cases the distance was 400 kilometres and the results were telegraphed. Sometimes the average was ten instead of five. One can well understand Rhine's confidence in asserting that he has proved the existence of psychic powers in ordinary people. Packs of these cards can be bought in the bookshops of America so people can conduct their own experiments.

If the question is asked: Are there many people with pronounced psychic powers like the former well-known mediums, the answer must be, No. The days of the great mediums are over. The only *showpiece* known to parapsychological circles is a Dutch practitioner named Gerard Croiset. He has often been tested scientifically by Professor Tenhaeff (Utrecht) and Professor Bender (Freiburg) who are of the opinion that he is a genuine clairvoyant.

Let us look at an example of his art which has been described by Anton Neuhäusler, tutor in philosophy at Munich University. Croiset wrote in Utrecht a series of statements that were supposed to apply to definite people attending a seance. This seance took place later on in Munich. The forty-nine people present had not all been invited by the same person. They were all interested in taking part in an experiment to discover the *statistical probability of chance statements*. It turned out that one set of his statements fitted with remarkable accuracy the leader of the seance whom Croiset had seen only once for a short time in Stuttgart without knowing anything about him. The reader must judge for himself whether the statements offer proof, or are of such a general nature that they could have been the result of probability or sheer luck. One case supported by strong proof is more valuable than any number of vague ones for finding out the truth of these phenomena. Confirmation or correction is given here by Anton Neuhäusler in brackets following Croiset's statement.

1. A person who is peremptory and speaks emphatically and is a man of few words. (People who know him say this describes him exactly.)

3. I see a woman of Marie-Antoinette's time . . . Has he this week or recently been talking about the eighteenth century? (He had been talking to his wife about Marie-Antoinette and the eighteenth century.)

4. He occasionally suffers from pains in the region of the heart with congestion and feelings of depression about which he worries now and then. (He had been thinking of going to the doctor for some time.)

8. (a) Velocitas . . . What does it mean? (He was working on an essay on relativity and was having difficulty over the idea of velocity.)

In addition to making statements of this kind, Croiset predicts which person will sit on a certain seat at a lecture and adds details about him or her such as "a lady who has just bought a new hat", and so on. Here he is astonishingly accurate.

Like many other clairvoyants he also goes in for psychometry, i.e. he takes a ring or watch in his hand and can make statements about the owner or wearer. The conclusion must not be drawn, however, that the object gives out electric waves or possesses an "atmosphere", a kind of fluid or aura or odour as many parapsychologists have thought. There is no evidence for it in my opinion, although some claim that there is.

Reports of such radiation from spirit personalities are of course always cropping up. They come especially from India and in our own western culture from anthroposophical societies. Many think this is the origin of the halo. But are there really any rays which are only visible to the initiated? It may or may not be so. Most parapsychologists assert that it is the object itself which stirs the clairvoyant's subconscious into activity. Astonishing cases have been reported. Tischner writes of a Mr. H. who had a tightly wrapped parcel pressed into his hand and made the following statement: "Lady dressed in pink. She has a chain round her neck, a necklace, pearls with something like a star or cross attached. Now it is a cross. Lady of about thirty, mature lady, light red hair, very proud face." The packet contained a rosary that had been blessed by the Pope. The shape of the object inside was perfectly recognised though the description was not so clear. The owner of the rosary agreed that she was very proud.

Some months later I handed the same object to the clairvoyant again. He said at once "I see the Pope, a shining white appearance". This incident assumed a quite different aspect almost a year later. Happening to take up the rosary, I discovered a small magnifying glass concealed in the centre of the cross, through which a picture of the Pope in a white silk dress could be seen. Many souvenirs have this kind of magnifying glass. The clairvoyant had seen through the paper wrapping a minute glass which one had to look through very sharply in order to see the tiny picture of the Pope. That would indeed be a striking proof of clairvoyance if it conformed to all the conditions of scientific control.

Critical Considerations

With this question of honest testing we enter the realm of criticism. Here the critics are to be given a chance to speak with more seriousness and thoroughness than is found in many descriptions.

It is well to point out first of all that there are certain areas where clairvoyance, or second sight as it is sometimes called, occurs relatively often. Scotland is one; the Lüneburger Heide with its *Spökenkieker* (seers of ghosts) is another. I also found one in the Mainhardt Forest and Löwenstein mountains of North

Würtenberg. People living to the west of the Neckar, however, are more rational and commonsense in their thinking. It is interesting to find that there are chemical causes for this. A folklorist named Schmeïng has shown that lack of calcium in the water favours clairvoyance and vice versa.

Is second sight a genuine gift or is it merely the effect of a strong imagination? Cannot this phenomenon, which is endemic to a particular area, be likened to the infection spread by a stimulating personality who groups round him a circle of believers? They suddenly undergo a mass experience of a supernatural nature, as with the patients of Dr. Charcot in Paris, where contortions, shrieks and other signs of hysteria were the order of the day. Is it not a fact that many people are only too ready to believe in the sensational and marvellous but not interested enough to submit them to critical examination?

Another word that is used as an objection is chance. Not used in its deeper, cosmic sense but as it is used in normal everyday affairs. For example, I arrive five minutes late for a train that happens that day to be eight minutes late, so I am lucky enough to be able to catch it. Critics maintain that it is the same with second sight. A thousand people may dream of an accident. If one happens in reality, the other 999 cases are forgotten. Croiset makes a whole series of depositions, some right, some half right and some wrong. But only the few right ones arouse astonishment. What man of fifty who feels the strain of his professional work does not occasionally find something abnormal about his heart? What woman has never bought a white blouse or, if it was in fashion, a blue hat? As soon as a statement can be regarded as a lucky shot, it is no longer specific nor has it any significance, i.e. it proves nothing.

The word chance raises many problems. In his valuable book *Chance and Fate*, Wilhelm von Scholz maintains that there are not only stupid and trifling cases of chance but also sensible ones intimately bound up in some mysterious way with fate. C. G. Jung has developed this idea in his book on *Synchronicity as a Principle of Non-causal Connections* (1952). According to this theory, if a fire is raging in Stockholm and Swedenborg sees it from a far distant town, this is not caused by the fire. There is a higher reality from the standpoint of which time and space are seen to be relative. This reality directs the two events *sympathetically* so that the spirit can rise above time and space. Such a novel idea needs to be thought out and tested.

But let us return to simpler modes of thought. Here mention must be made of the clarifying work of Wilhelm Gubisch, though he gets on the nerves of many believers in occultism and even of parapsychologists. In many of his lecture-experiments, mostly given to doctors and crime specialists, he pretends for the first half of the evening to have second sight and makes statements that reveal secret knowledge, just like a genuine clairvoyant. In the second half he demonstrates how he arrived at this knowledge in quite normal ways, i.e. through psychological perception, clever guessing, tentative and vague statements and casual questions thrown in now and again. The luck of a chance shot always helps.

I myself was present when he told a simple-minded man that he had a cupboard in his bedroom (as had 95 per cent of the audience!); on its floor there were some boxes with some small round objects in them. They were coins from a small collection. This last was the *significant* remark. The man agreed that it was so and the experiment was a success. Gubisch says this statement is part of his standard programme. Twenty years ago he published an account in which this and other standard statements like "birthmark on the right hip" find a place. Gubisch therefore denies the existence of psychic powers. It is not the clairvoyant who makes the phenomenon remarkable but the credulous public who are always ready to believe anything.

Here it may be said that many world-famous cases of true, specific statements which appeared to be valid at the time, have not stood up to closer critical examination. One such case is the prophetic dream of Bishop Lanyi. On June 28th, 1914, at four o'clock in the morning, he dreamt every detail of the brutal assassination of the Archduke of Austria at Serajevo. At about seven o'clock he related his dream to his servant, his mother and a guest. After detailed research Gubisch proves from correspondence with all the persons concerned who are still alive, that this model example cannot, unfortunately, be true. There is of course a manuscript copy of the dream but it could only have been written after the death of the Archduke. Besides, several important details of the real occurrence are missing. There was only one assassin, not two, as the dream described. The other was elsewhere at the time. The chief woman witness on whom the telling of the dream should have made an indelible impression for the rest of her life, wrote to say that the bishop was very nervously wrought at the time. She had entirely forgotten whether he had spoken about the dream on the day they received the news or the day after. Furthermore it must be remembered that many had advised the Archduke and his wife against making the journey for fear of an attempt on their lives. The bishop was very much taken up with his dreaming and, according to one of his fellow-countrymen who was an Archbishop, had a very lively imagination. We must therefore rule this case out from the literature on the subject. It casts doubt on many other well-known examples.

Another objection to the reality of supra-sensitive perception is raised against the value to be attached to J. B. Rhine's experiments. It is not only disputed whether they took place in unexceptionable scientific conditions without the possibility of error, but experts like Otto Prokop, formerly of the Institute of Law and Psychology in Bonn and now professor at the Humboldt University in East Berlin, who believe in psychic perception, consider Rhine's method insufficient. Tornier, professor of mathematics at Göttingen University writes: "Personally I regard the existence of telepathy, clairvoyance and precognition as proved by many experiences: so I am not against parapsychology. What I am against is his method of mathematical proof which is obviously false."

If we give due weight to all these objections, we must, in all honesty, admit that it is not yet definite whether clairvoyance exists or not. Either the results are meagre or the method is dubious. Even in spontaneous cases like the Bishop's we must be on our guard. It is clear that there is much prejudice both for and against occult phenomena. Many flatly deny that there is anything abnormal or mysterious about such things. There are, however, some spontaneous cases that are so remarkable that they deserve further examination.

Soothsaying and Fortune-telling

More important than the scientific problem is the cosmic one. And here it must be strongly emphasised that affirmations of faith have nothing to do with the reality of clairvoyance. Just as you cannot prove the existence of God scientifically, so you cannot conclude from the accomplishment of some psychic prediction that there is a supernatural world. The most successful examples still leave us within the limits of our earthly existence. We have at best discovered a new and mysterious side to our human nature or, as Edgar Dacqué suggests, re-discovered powers of the mind we possessed long ago. However interesting and remarkable they are, they will not change our lives. Even if they did we should not stop going about our daily work and using our brains to plan the future. Who wants to rely every day on ghosts who never give us a whole picture of reality but only chance fragments of it? That is not the way for people who, as Christ says, are to be "workers and wise householders". On the contrary when we meet Christians who show far too great an interest in psychic phenomena, we are entitled to ask whether their devoutness is healthy and whether their faith is really in "the evidence of things not seen" (Heb. 11: 1). Gubisch was right when he said that the genuinely religious person had no need of the occult.

Many Christians may ask: Are there not numerous examples of prophecy in the Bible? Did not the prophets foresee the future? Did not Christ foretell the fall of Jerusalem?

All this is certainly true, but we must make a sharp distinction between the prophecies in the Bible and those of clairvoyance and soothsaying. A prophet is not primarily a foreteller of the future. He is God's plenipotentiary and ambassador extraordinary who is sent to the people of his day to call them back to God. "Repent and change!" That is the burden of the prophet's call. He only unfolds the threatened judgments which God has revealed to him in order to rouse his lazy and cocksure contemporaries.

This is the characteristic difference between the clairvoyant and the prophet. The former talks about trifles and things of importance in one and the same breath, according to the haphazard images that come up into his mind. The prophet, on the other hand, is interested in social and political affairs, a pastor who loves his nation ardently, who reflects upon the evils of his time, is wise with the wisdom of this world and understands power politics. His anxieties, fears and political outlook are co-ordinated and heightened by the voice of God who speaks mightily to him and he simply passes it on. One has only to read the first chapter of Isaiah to see straight away what a difference there is between him and the clairvoyant with a private practice who has only spontaneous experiences or, like Croiset, makes political and religious remarks of no importance.

Of course it must be admitted that in addition to this line of genuine prophets there is a second group in the Bible. In the period after the exile (586-539 B.C.), it is noticeable that more interest is shown in foretelling the future in detail and more use is made of sacred numbers. This apocalyptic interest can be seen in the Book of Daniel and the Book of Revelation. But these secondary matters must not be given the prime importance that Jehovah's Witnesses and other sects give them. Neither book must be used as an oracle by which to discover the future. They must still remain as God's genuine words of exhortation and appeal, of comfort and warning for all generations of Christians. This is an instance of the difference between prophecy and fortune-telling.

In view of this distinction the objections of some philosophers, even against genuine prophecy, carry no weight. They maintain that if a prophecy works out, it is because it had been decided upon beforehand, which means that there is no such thing as the lapse of time; in some fourth dimension everything that we call future is present. Furthermore man is robbed of all freedom, responsibility and chance to plan his world; he is a mere automaton who must follow the course of things as they have already been laid down. It only *seems* as though man has freedom of choice.

We do not need here to go into this 2,000-year-old dispute between determinism and indeterminism (or fatalism and free will). The Christian does not look upon God as impersonal law that prescribes an unalterable course. For the believer He is the personal, free, creative Lord who does indeed plan and who wavers not, but can at any time alter His plan for individuals. That is the real meaning of the biblical phrase: "it repented Him". Such an expression, far from giving a primitive picture of a god-man, represents His supreme freedom and mercy. In reality it may seem indeed as if everything, including man and his decisions, have to keep to a blind law of cause and effect, but looked at from the point of view of faith, the world is at every moment new in God's hands and everything depends on whether I accept God's will and decisions. This the man who runs to clairvoyants and soothsayers in order to find out the future does not want to do. Instead of doing his duty in obedience to what God's commandments say and trusting God for the future, he wants to be like God, hold the future in his hands and be master of his fate.

Suppose a successful clairvoyant tells a soldier he will return safely from the war. The man is no longer a poor, fearful yet hopeful creature who has to put his trust in God. He has become lord over his own fate. He has his return ticket in his pocket, has seen behind the scenes in the government of the world and feels safe. But that is precisely the fatal pride of man that wars against the overlordship of God. For this reason going to soothsayers and clairvoyants, unless it be for purposes of scientific investigation, is for the Christian, not only stupidity, not only a waste of money, but a sin against the first commandment which says "I am the Lord thy God; thou shalt have none other gods beside me". God alone has the right to a capital G. He who gives us everything we possess wills to be Lord not only of our present but also of our future. Therefore faith rejects as superstition every purely human attempt to gain a supernatural and supra-sensitive look into the future.

4

Dream and Reality

WE have met with dreams in the previous chapter. Clairvoyant experiences may, of course, take place in the conscious mind, in a trance or in a dream, but the subject of dreams deserves a chapter to itself. Interpreting dreams goes back to the earliest times. From ancient Egypt to the present day it has exercised an important influence on the history of man. The instances in the Bible are of varying value.

Historical Account of Dream Interpretation

The word dream sounds a warning note. It comes from the Teutonic word *draugma,* meaning an illusory picture. The German proverb: "Dreams are Shadows", and the French one which runs "Dreams are Lies" express a healthy scepticism.

Man has been preoccupied with his dreams from earliest times. Nomads and hunters often had interrupted sleep due to their manner of life and the hostility of their surroundings. Every morning they woke up with their dreams still fresh in their minds. Their sense of reality was not yet sufficiently developed to enable them to distinguish between waking and dreaming. It is said that they were only able to enjoy longer periods of sleep when they had tamed the dog.

In *Gilgamish,* the Babylonian epic, we find great value attached to dreams and in Egypt dream interpretation had been worked out to a fine art. The Royal Palace School established a special faculty for it. Verse eight of the forty-first chapter of Genesis might be translated as "Scribes of the House of Life". These were highly respected soothsayers and wise men in Pharaoh's household. They belonged mostly to the nobility.

Their dream interpretation was closely related to the ideas the Egyptians had of the world around them. Like the Babylonians, they believed the visible world was surrounded by a heaven of water called *Nun.* Every night the sun god was supposed to dive into this water and refresh himself for the next day. In the same way it was thought that man plunges into the night of sleep and there comes into contact with the heavenly world where the gods and ancestors live who replenish him with wisdom. Hence the belief that dreams were true.

Because dreams were so highly regarded, special techniques were worked out for producing them artificially. People prayed and fasted, shut themselves up in caves, or slept in temples as they do today in Japan. Others submitted to initiation ceremonies conducted by the priests and drank intoxicating liquors such as henbane and thornapple. Later on people smoked opium and hashish.

Such means were also used at the sacred oracle in Delphi in Greece. The prophetess sat on a tripod above a crack in the ground from which rose hypnotising gases which sent the prophetess into a trance. She then uttered confused sounds and meaningless sentences, like the lama in Tibet. Skilled and clever priests then interpreted them for their clients.

Next to the observatory on the huge step pyramid in Babylon known as the Tower of Babel there was a room which contained a golden statue of the god Marduk. At the New Year a specially chosen maiden spent the night in it and was visited by the gods. Her dream was supposed to foretell what would happen to the country in the course of the year.

Dreams were also connected with the healing of disease. People who were ill went to Serapion in Lower Egypt, where they were told in a dream the right medicine to take and the right treatment. In other places the goddess Isis graciously appeared to the patients and gave them an elixir.

Whilst Homer, and at times the Pythagoreans too, lived in this world of dreams, the golden age of Greek culture was once again on the way to finding a new conception of reality and scientific criticism. Aristotle, who lived about 350 B.C., thought dreams were only the continuation in sleep of the waking activity of the mind, as if seen through rippling water. One had only to know how these distorted images could be straightened out. The contents of a dream were not to be interpreted as indications of the future communicated by the gods, but to the workings of the human mind within the sphere of the natural world. He had the ingenious idea that *inner perception* is heightened in a dream and can give fore-warning of an illness whose painful symptoms are not yet being felt by the dreamer in his waking moments. Cicero makes a delightful criticism from the rational point of view in his *De Divinatione*. He suggests that it would be more dignified of the gods if they appeared to people when they were awake instead of to the snorers among whom the scoffers are to be found.

In the twilight of declining oriental civilisation, these practices sank lower and lower. The greatest interpreter of dreams in the ancient world was Artemidorus who lived about 180 B.C. in Daldis near Ephesus. Even he includes in his five-volume work, among many surprisingly accurate psychological observations, a wealth of superstitious ideas gathered from Babylonian, Egyptian and other sources. Books on dreams degenerated into senseless casuistry. Blood meant money; a wedding dress stood for death; fire meant a wedding; a raven an adulterer, while among the Egyptians a crocodile stood for a rapacious official!

During the Middle Ages this kind of dream interpretation came into the West via the Arabs who also brought astrology with them. Mistakes in translating their books added to the misunderstandings and confusion, so that modern buyers and sellers of *genuine* Egyptian books on dreams are often themselves the victims of a real *draugma* or delusion.

Psychoanalysis and Dream Interpretation

In heathen religions every dream was connected in some way or another with the world of the gods. Modern psychology on the other hand starts from different premises. It seeks to explain the significance of dreams by reference to man's human nature. In the last century, when mechanistic ideas were the prevailing fashion, chief emphasis was laid on proving that dreams were caused by external stimuli.

This may often be true. The so-called nightmares are not caused by goblins or elves sitting on our chests but by eating too much supper! The famous experiment carried out by Hildebrandt (1875), however, shows how small the influence of an external stimulus can be. On one occasion the ringing of his alarm bell made him dream of church bells on a Sunday morning. On another occasion it made him dream of the tinkling of sleigh bells. The third time he saw a kitchen maid in front of him drop a pile of plates with a loud crash. The important thing about these dreams is not the external stimulus but the state of mind of the dreamer.

We are reminded here of the pioneer work of Sigmund Freud (1856-1939), the founder of psychoanalysis. He reduced to a scientific system what the German Romantics and Nietzsche had vaguely divined and gave us the modern view of human personality. His work is comparable in importance to that of Copernicus in astronomy. His main idea has been already mentioned in chapter one; here we must go more deeply into it.

According to Freud we should no longer regard consciousness as the essential mark of a human being. It is only like a thin skin, the surface covering the deep ocean of the subconscious which is populated with numberless monsters, some larger, some smaller, but all at war with each other. These are the urges, desires and passions which reside in the depths of the human psyche of even the best of men. Only a precarious superstructure connects him to the higher world of ideals, of justice, kindness and sympathy. These ideals, which have been mostly inculcated in the children by the older, ruling generation, exercise a kind of censorship. Any primitive urge that seeks to issue in action is pushed back into the subconscious. There it forms a complex deep down which later on makes a new attempt to work its way into the conscious mind. If any severe conflict arises, psychoses and neuroses are formed. Even the spiritual balance of so-called sound people is always unsteady and highly vulnerable.

Freud rejected out of hand the beatings, strait jackets, drugs, baths or electric shock with which the mentally ill were treated in order to restore them to normal. He recommended, and himself practised, the healing effect of a quiet talk with a doctor who then cautiously probes into the patient's subconscious, gets to where the complex started, brings it up into the conscious and so resolves it. Freud called the remembering and relating of dreams the "royal road" into the subconscious, for during dreams the psyche succumbs to the powers of the subconscious unprotected by the superstructure, the idealist ego.

These fundamental ideas have now become the basis of modern psychology. Two of his characteristic theories, however, have been hotly disputed. The first is that the main content of the subconscious is the libido, the sex urge, taken, of course, in its widest sense. The second is that the child is in the main father to the man; and the man can only be understood by exploring his earliest recollections of childhood. Placed as he is between his parents, he is suppressed by their overriding power and forced to assert himself. He has already received from one or the other the *trauma* (wound) from which he will suffer all his life. This is the explanation of the famous Oedipus complex. According to the legend, Oedipus slew his father in ignorance and married his mother. Freud maintains that the boy was unconsciously jealous of his father and burned with sexual passion for his mother.

For Freud this conception illuminated as in a flash the darkness which had hitherto concealed the true meaning of dreams. He made a start with daydreams in which we let our minds run on and our hopes and fears and desires pass before us.

From all this he drew up the following rules for interpreting daydreams.

1. Every dream has a meaning. It always says something about the character and personality of the dreamer, about his joys and sorrows, his motives and aims.

2. A distinction must be drawn between the meaning of the dream and the pictures it conjures up. What we experience in the dream is only a distorted substitute for what the subconscious is really after. Our waking consciousness and our idealist ego have already exercised some control and only allow a censored image to come to the surface, i.e. into our memory. For example, a young man dreamt several nights on end about a small dog and could not think why. Then it occurred to him he had seen this dog when he had met a young lady who had made a very great impression on him. He had not wanted to think any more about her, as there were various reasons why a closer association was out of the question. But his liking for her had simmered on in his subconscious mind and had tried to come to the surface again. In his dream only the small dog who had happened to be with the girl appeared. It had nothing to do with the real meaning of the dream or with the conflict going on in the dreamer's mind.

3. Out of this continual struggle between the conscious and the subconscious, between the ego and the mind, arises what Freud calls *dreamwork*. The dream dramatises the conflict and compresses it into one situation, or it transfers it from place to place, or again by its very nature it transforms abstract thoughts into visual images. The idea of a broken marriage is changed into the loss of a wedding ring, as in Justinus Kerner's folk song *Mein Ringlein ist zerbrochen* (My ring has broken).

4. As human anxieties and needs are mostly the same the world over, it has been possible in the course of time to draw up a dream language of its own, a particular *Symbolism*, which holds good for any language or people. They are mostly of a sexual nature. (Freud laid great stress on the sex urge). A tower, a stick, a rod, a knife or a revolver represent a man. A house, a cave, a cell, water, bushes, a pot or an old box may all represent a woman. Climbing, falling, fighting, defeat, swimming or flying represent the sex act or some such excitement.

5. As we said above, Freud believed that childhood's impressions were in most cases of decisive importance. Many dreams can be traced back to a wounding of the child's spirit or they reflect a situation in the early life of the child. A man who now loves his grown-up brother, may, after many years, experience

again in a dream the desire he had at the age of three to murder him for stealing the affection of the parents.

Psychoanalysts say that many anxiety dreams (anxiety means narrow by derivation), refer to the time of birth which is often associated with a frightening experience of distress or confinement. Many dreams in which swimming occurs, and even the fairy story of the stork pond in which unborn children are supposed to swim are said to be based on a pre-natal memory of the embryo swimming in the amniotic fluid with which it is surrounded. It is not for nothing that Freud prefaced his book on dream interpretation (1900) with the words *Acheronta movebo* (I will stir up the underworld).

It is well known today that many anxiety dreams are attributable to mistakes in the way parents bring up their children. To threaten a baby too severely or too suddenly gives its defenceless heart a shock which causes it to dream years after. It may dream that it is running away, or standing naked or in its nightshirt in front of people on the platform of a railway station.

Freud's ideas, brilliant though they are, have been criticised in recent years, even by some of his students. Alfred Adler (1870-1937) opposed his over-emphasis of sex. For Adler, sex is not the central urge in a man's life. The urge to be at the centre of things, to raise his own status is stronger. It might be called the *will to power*. The clue to man's nature is not found by looking backwards at its causes, but rather taking a forward look at the leading, subconscious idea that governs his ultimate aims and purposes. In interpreting dreams one should not ask, Why did I dream this? but, For what purpose did I dream it?

The world-famous Zürich scholar C. G. Jung (1877-1961) added to and changed some of these ideas. He was the son of a Swiss pastor and came of a line of pastors and doctors. By his discovery of the deep level of the collective unconscious, he extended the pattern of the human personality and superseded Freud's dream symbolism. In the depths of the psyche slumber the *archetypes*, primitive images of universal human nature, homogeneous constructions which appear again and again in dreams and show not only relationships to parents, sex relationships, the struggle for existence, but also something positive in the ethical sense: symbols of change and maturity, of the image of God and death. In addition to slight dreams which concern only the individual, there are great dreams which concern humanity as a whole. Jung attributed special importance to the so-called *Mandala* symbol (from Sanskrit meaning a circle), the symbol of man's striving after self-realisation and full perfection. Freud based his observations on a decadent society within the environment of one great city and so over-stressed the sex element and broke down the integrated personality. Jung on the other hand, always finds in man's deepest self the will to health, the will to maturity and even an experience of God. So with him psychiatry becomes more human and rises from the mire of an underworld which, all the same, is very real.

On this point, Professor Bender quotes a good example from Jung's book *The Reality of the Psyche*. A young man dreams that his father drives away from the house in a new car. His steering is very unsteady and he runs into a wall. The young man then notices that his father is drunk. This dream clearly gives a very unfavourable picture of the father. Restricted to a theory which regards the unconscious as concerned only with things that are negative or destructive, one would be inclined to reduce this dream to some unconscious aggression against the father and see in it the young man's real relationship to him. Neither the ideas, the amplification of the dream nor the actual situation in real life gave the slightest suspicion of such an interpretation. The meaning became clear when the purpose of the dream was investigated. Obviously the young man's unconscious wants to take the father down a peg or two. Judged from the point of view of compensation, this leads to the conclusion that the boy's relationship to his father was not only good, but too good. He depends too much on his father whom he feels to be his superior and so does not learn to stand on his own feet. So the unconscious has recourse to an artificial blasphemy by which to bring the father down and raise the son up, contrasting him favourably with the father he admires. The young man agreed at once with this interpretation.

Dreams then help the process of individuation, of growing up. As Jung says, the boy ought to honour his father but he should also learn to be independent and go his own way.

This method of interpretation disproves Freud's idea that a dream has a definite picture that can be firmly outlined. It is rather a groping of the self after an understanding of human relationships, in which case it is not necessary to work out an interpretation for every dream. Some are best forgotten, though Jung regards a conversation with any dreamer about the meaning, aims and content of his life as providing valuable enlightenment.

Dreams in the Bible

Psychological explanations may be all very well for ordinary dreams, but what about the numerous dreams in the Bible? Are they only to be taken in a psychological sense or has the one true God spoken to men in dreams? Such a question cannot be answered with a short yes or no. We see, even in the Bible, various lines to be distinguished.

The Old Testament is as full of dreams as its contemporary world. Mention need only be made of Jacob's beautiful dream of the ladder set up to heaven which gave him the certainty that God had chosen him (Genesis 28). If we think too of Joseph the dreamer and the meaning of his dreams, we see how similar they were to dreams in the pagan world which foretold future greatness to the elect. Pharaoh's dreams have a significance that is peculiar to Egypt. The seven fat kine and the seven lean kine meant years, because the hieroglyphic for cow and year is the same. It must be agreed that certain biblical dreams are as purely selfish as heathen ones. They seek too much after good luck in spite of a deeper hidden sense of mission which they certainly possess, e.g. Genesis 31: 10 ff.

There is a difference between these parts of the Old Testament and the religions of the other tribes. There is nothing trivial or sexual about them. This is due to the predominant figure of God who rules over history and is Himself holy and above all worlds. Man cannot here control his dreams in the way the magicians do. To want to do so leads straight to superstition. Like Joseph, he says in humble faith: "Do not interpretations belong unto God?" (Gen. 40: 8). Daniel expresses the same thought centuries later. When the wise men and learned soothsayers in Babylon were unable to interpret the dream, Daniel says: "But there is a God in heaven that revealeth secrets and maketh known to king Nebuchadnezzar what shall be in the latter days" (Dan. 2: 28). The Lord of history can use dreams for His purposes when He needs to.

This attitude to dreams is not met with everywhere in the Old Testament. The major prophets, from their purely moral and spiritual standpoint, are clearly distrustful of them. In one of the sources of the first five books of the Bible, the so-called *priestly* writings, it is characteristic that the Lord does not speak to Moses in dreams, but directly by word of mouth (Num. 12: 6 ff.). The prophet Jeremiah in particular opposed the priests of his time who dabbled in dreams. He turns in righteous anger on those soothsayers who prophesied out of the deceptions of their own hearts. "The prophet that hath a dream, let him tell a dream; and he that hath my word, let him speak my word faithfully. What is the chaff to the wheat? saith the Lord" (Jer. 23: 28).

This clearly means that the word of God comes to the conscious mind of the prophet as he wrestles in dialogue with God; whereas the dreams he talks of arise only in the subconscious of the dreamer.

The books of Wisdom, which are of a later date, also reject dreams. But here the attitude is one of scepticism due to a more rational outlook on the world. "For in the multitude of dreams and many words there are also diverse vanities; but fear thou God" (Ecclesiastes 5: 7). cf. Ecclesiasticus 34.

It is worthy of note that in the New Testament the word dream only occurs twice—in Matthew and the Acts. These dreams, however, are more like visions which convey the direct guidance of God. They are connected more with hearing than with seeing. In the historically important vision that Paul had on the shores of Asia Minor (Acts 16), it does not say that he was asleep. In his short autobiography (2 Cor. 11 and 12), he makes no mention of any dreams and speaks only under compulsion of his visions and revelations from the Lord.

The reason why the New Testament is so sparing in its reference to dreams is that the Christians were not actuated by greed or fear but were living under a sense of being guided by God and strengthened by Him. Albrecht Oepke maintains that every account of a dream in the New Testament is some variation of the central theme of Christ. This is in line with the fact that no one has a frightening dream with the exception of the pagan wife of Pilate (Matt. 27: 19). Oepke further adds that the conflict between superstition and reason in the ancient world was resolved on a higher plane by faith and trust in the living God.

Findings

How do these two ways of considering dreams, the psychological and the biblical, affect our attitude towards their interpretation? Our findings can be summed up in a few sentences.

1. Christians should be aware of the difficulties connected with a purely psychological method of interpretation. There are different schools of thought. Their interpretations depend on how they view the world and what premises they adopt.

2. Christians should not take their dreams too seriously. Most of our dreams are of the slight kind and are made up of a mixture of daylight happenings that our minds have not fully taken in.

3. Many of our dreams we cannot remember properly. They get confused and altered in the telling without our really mean-

ing to do so. This process shows, of course, that we are still imprisoned in our little selves.

4. We should not emphasise the many parts of the Bible that have something in common with older religions, but concentrate rather on those prophets who, by the clarity of their thinking, give us word and answer and by their intelligent service to God set before us the Lord of our lives. Searching out what is mysterious, strange or extraordinary is no special sign of piety. We should remember how Paul praises love above extraordinary gifts of the spirit, as *the more excellent way*. (1 Cor. 13).

5. Where God does give guidance through a dream, who are we to deny Him the freedom to choose what means He likes? As regards our own genuine dreams, we should be very cautious and bear in mind what has been said in a previous chapter about the unreliability and ambiguities of clairvoyance.

Being a Christian means being matter of fact. It means prayer and work (*Ora et labora*). Christ did not say, sleep and pray nor, we may add, dream and pray, but "Watch and pray that ye enter not into temptation". In the end, what is fruitful is not introspection or deep self-concern, but looking up to the Lord on high.

5

Ghosts, Hauntings and Spiritism

THERE is an Icelandic legend which tells the story of some young Vikings who went out on a war expedition. After many weeks on stormy seas they returned home laden with rich booty. On the way they passed, at dead of night, the place where their grandsire, Thorleif, was buried. They saw the burial mound open and their ancestor seated on a throne singing joyfully because he was so proud of his grandchildren. Long after they had gone past, they still heard his song of jubilation.

People who lived before Christ, with the exception of most of the Jews, did not regard death as being the end of earthly existence. The dead were believed to live on in the tribe and take part in its fortunes. They blessed and protected their descendants and lived in close community with them.

At the same time they were a source of fear and terror. People dreaded lest they might come back in bodily form as greedy spirits who would try to kill them so as to recover the power to live again. In the story of *Goden Snorri*, Thorold, a wicked man who was lame, has died on his throne in the banqueting hall. His people made a hole in the wall, crept up to him from behind and dragged him through it with every measure of precaution. After he had been buried, he returned as a ghost and haunted the district to everyone's terror. They dug up his body and buried it in a new grave, all to no effect. They dug him up again and burnt him. This was effective and peace was restored. In such desperate cases the ashes were scattered in a desert place where no one ever went.

This fear explains many of the burial customs. The dead man is beheaded or impaled. His body is mangled or drowned in a bog. The original purpose of the gravestone was not to commemorate the dead or even to protect them from wild animals, but to prevent them getting out of the grave!

This two-fold relationship to the dead can be seen in the religions of Egypt and the Middle East. The mysterious riddle of death provokes reverence, fear and curiosity. The fate of the dead exercises a fascinating attraction. It lies at the root of many of the reports of encounters with them through apparitions and haunting.

It is pertinent here to enquire seriously into what error and superstition are. What is the truth about ghosts and haunting? What has the Christian religion to say about them?

In order to get a comprehensive view of this complicated problem, we must proceed step by step from what is mere deception to such phenomena as have some grounds of proof of life after death. Then we must enquire what Christianity has to say.

Spiritist Sects

I should assign the lowest stage to spiritism. This movement began with some strange happenings which occurred about 1848 in the small town of Hydesville in New York State. The house in which John D. Fox was living with his three daughters was haunted. Inexplicable sounds were heard like tapping which seemed to come sometimes from the bedroom, sometimes from the cellar and sometimes from footsteps in different rooms. On one occasion the nine-year-old daughter felt a cold hand on her face. After a time, they thought they had got to the bottom of the trouble and tried to get into touch with the person. It turned out that a trader had been murdered in the house and his soul could find no rest. They dug in the cellar and found bits of bone and part of a skull. Confirmation of the remarkable occurrences, however, was not forthcoming till 1904, when a wall of the cellar fell in. This uncovered a hitherto unknown cavity in which there was the headless skeleton of a man.

The spiritist movement was started by the Fox sisters. In many circles and lodges table-rapping was eagerly practised and spirits called up. The sisters made a lot of money out of their detailed knowledge of the spirit world. In 1888, however, they admitted, even in their lectures, that they had made use of tricks and makeshifts. All the same, there was something genuine about the original event, as we shall see. But that does not alter the fact that these spiritist circles had all the typical traits of a sect: concentration on one main theme, lack of any critical examination of their belief, superiority over those who don't agree and a lust for ever more and more signs and wonders.

The sect spread with amazing rapidity at a time when there was a great lack of faith. There are six thousand lodges in North America, three hundred in England and a large number in Germany. South America, where the movement has millions of adherents, is known as the "spiritist continent". Karl Hutten estimates the world membership at fifty millions. They meet two or three times a week and assemble as if going to divine service, or to some substitute for it. They darken the room, sing hymns and sit in a circle holding hands. A medium falls into a trance and claims to summon the spirits of the dead. These are usually confined to friends and relatives, but sometimes well-known personalities of the past seem to appear and converse with those present. The following incidents from a Berlin Lodge show that there is sometimes an amusing breakdown.

On this occasion the participants were in a literary mood and the medium called up the spirit of Heinrich Heine, who seemed delighted to leave the underworld and be at their disposal. His shadowy figure appeared in the background and he imparted his wisdom through the mouth of the medium. On being asked if he would recite one of his poems, he declared himself quite willing. To the astonishment of everyone he recited with great fervour and in Berlin dialect, Schiller's *Hymn to Joy*, instead of his own poem *Die Lorelei*!

At another seance the great Arab prophet Mohammed was called up. He readily gave information about the oil crisis in Abadan and the love affairs of the Shah of Persia. As it happened a member of the Persian Embassy in Bonn was present. He was allowed to put a question to Mohammed. Instead of putting it in German, he put it in Persian and asked, "Nen udnen nabba?" Mohammed, who had been so ready to talk before, made no answer. On the question being repeated, he vanished.

After the seance the Persian remarked to a woman who was with him, "A remarkable man, this Mohammed. Either he has forgotten his native language or he can't count." "What did you ask him?" she said. "I asked him quite simply what twice two made," replied the Persian laughing.

Of course there are some earnest seekers among the spiritists, but the average level attained by their efforts would be adequately characterised by the experiments I have mentioned.

Illusions and Hallucinations

There are however some who are firmly convinced that their experiences with spirits are based on reality and they seek neither recognition nor money for it. Heinrich Ohlhaver is a good example. His book, *The Dead Live!* with its triumphant exclamation mark, has nearly reached the million mark. About 1900 this former business man was communicating with his late father as if he were still living. He and his medium, Elisabeth Tambke, lived in constant touch with the dead. The son is allowed to embrace his dead father and stroke his sidewhiskers. He feels the prickly hair as distinctly as during his father's last years on earth.

Do we learn from these spirits what it is like in the world beyond? This is surely one of the most serious questions that agitate the mind of man. What answer do we get? A young girl who died at about the age of twenty, says this. "Dying is a painful process, for first of all you sink slowly into sleep and for a long time after the doctors and my relatives thought I was dead, I saw and felt what was going on round me. I lay alone in the cold, dark grave, and only after some time came shining forms to help me up and carry me to a bright and beautiful *Summerland,* where friendly spirits allotted me a large and beautiful house surrounded by a magnificent park with green meadows where stags and deer were feeding. In the mornings I take a bath and then go for a ride. After that I go to a library and read. Sometimes I listen to lectures in a large glass hall that flashes with red and green flames."

When she was asked who gave the lectures, she said that a man called Socrates from Greece had just given an interesting lecture on philosophy.

We are free to draw what picture we like of the other world, but such dreams are nothing more than a child's fantasies.

The same applies to the lectures given by spirits, such as you hear in seances in England. A lecture was given by a famous scholar named *Zodiac*—a highly improbable name from a historical point of view—who was supposed to have taught in the Temple at the time of Christ and to be identical with the scholar mentioned in Mark 12: 28 ff. What he said, however, consisted only of general statements decked out with moral sentiments suited to a smug bourgeoisie.

To this mass psychosis, which has been known about for a long time, has been added in recent years, another wild idea—the so-called flying saucers, unknown objects flying in the air. There is already a whole literature about them. One man solemnly explained to me that they were the spirits of pilots who fell in both world wars and could not rest, so they were still flying round in the skies! The American Air Force made careful investigations and found countless instances of faulty observation. Possible explanations included aerial mirages, cloud formations, high altitude winds, satellites, planes flying at a great height and even rockets sent up by foreign powers. Even sane and sensible observers were deceived.

The stories of a man named Adamski, who claimed to have sailed round the moon and Venus in a space ship, belong to the realm of fantasy. This "President of the World", who was destined by the inhabitants of Venus to rule our planet, collected a large number of subscriptions from his "subjects" to pay for his coronation. He is now reflecting on his dreams in prison.

C. G. Jung, with his great understanding of modern man, has pointed out that there lies something deeper behind all this.

There is in existence a report made by a Viennese family. They were cultured people who would scorn to tell a lie or make money out of these things. They all saw over the wooded mountains round Vienna three objects in the shape of saucers which moved and changed direction so quickly that they could not have been aeroplanes. (Diagram 5). The underside was sometimes

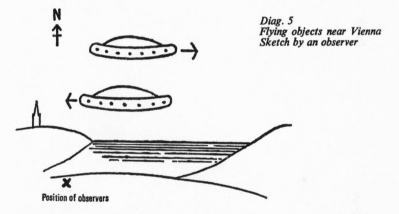

Diag. 5
Flying objects near Vienna
Sketch by an observer

Position of observers

bright red and sometimes green. Unfortunately they could neither be filmed nor recorded on tape, so they are not subject to proof.

How do people come to make this kind of statement? Jung has discovered two psychological reasons. Just as our remote ancestors were frightened of dragons and giants, so we today are frightened of atom bombs. Because we don't admit it, a fear complex forms in our universal subconscious mind. Some project this fear into the sky which they people with unknown beings whom they try every day to render harmless by wishfully dreaming of them as kind, friendly people who can remove fear from the earth and establish an age of peace. Hence the *gentle* inhabitants of Venus.

The second reason is that we stand today on the threshold of a new age. Infinitesimal man, who for millions of years has been confined to this earth, is now preparing to launch out into the yawning desolation of space. Whether he succeeds, or whether we shall be limited at most to the small area of our solar system does not excite the masses spiritually. Yet with many people this inner stirring, this stage fright before appearing on a different and larger world stage, leads to an externalisation. They regard space as being endowed with strange and superior powers.

It is characteristic that ideas of flying saucers should appear as early as the year one thousand, a significant date for those times, and in the stormy days of the Reformation and the Thirty Years' War. In times of crisis our complex human personality does a lot of imagining in order to preserve its balance.

Apart from any possible lurking deception behind phenomena of this kind, we feel that they are a matter of illusion. Professor Anschütz of Hamburg thinks they may be transposed, or erroneous explanations of things actually seen, in a word, hallucinations, i.e. images which do not exist in the visible world but arise in the observer and appear to him as if they came from outside him.

These hallucinations occur frequently among primitive peoples and among children between the ages of three and fourteen. According to the researches carried out by E. R. Jaensch and O. Kroh of Marburg, they are due to eidetism, or the gift of visualisation. Many authors like Schmeing trace the belief in survival after death to inner visual experiences of this kind. In the half light of their caves men saw a fallen comrade sitting again by the fire. The vision was born of their sorrow and longings. They were not able to distinguish this vision from reality. The savage is no more to be blamed for this than is a child at play who takes a piece of wood for a dog because it looks a bit like one.

Grown up, educated people of a higher culture, however, should be able to distinguish between fact and fancy. God gave this commission to man at the time of the creation (Gen. 1 : 28b). But there are people today, as in those days, and whole groups of them, who likewise cannot make this distinction. At some point their sense of reality fails them. At the same time they appear to be smitten with partial delusion, like members of some fanatical sect. Most of them are incurable. Every contradiction makes them more stubborn and the greater becomes the hold their false ideas have on them. Their horizon is limited entirely by this world. None of their dreams hint at another world order. None of these believers in flying saucers have ever said anything that better educated people or more serious seekers after truth would ever listen to. They live content with the world portrayed in the cheaper illustrated magazines which reflect only the fears and fancies of the less educated classes. What Max Dessoir says of mediums in the real sense of that word, applies to all announcers of other worlds: "The worlds described by the mediums are pitiable trash".

Telekinesis, Haunting and Poltergeists

We have seen how mediums brag and claim too much. In what follows we shall be dealing with simpler things but ones which have a greater content of probability. We meet here phenomena which have been recorded over and over again for centuries past. People hear, without any apparent natural cause, rattling, knocking or tramping in a room where they are sitting. A cold stream of air is felt. People imagine they have been touched or stroked. Plates and jugs fly through the air and either smash or come gently to rest on the floor. These things happen in broad daylight as well as at night. Even farm buildings are haunted. I was credibly informed of a place in the Mainhardt forest where the horses were found one morning in an extraordinary state: they were bathed in sweat and trembled all over. Their chains had been released and their manes and tails carefully plaited.

Many such cases have been described in detail and have become famous. From ancient Greece comes Pliny's story of a haunted house in Athens where the rattle of chains was heard repeatedly. There is a record from the year 1817 of a ghost that was seen for several weeks walking near Stallhofen in Steiermark. In her book on ghosts, Fanny Moser gives a detailed description of a Swiss Member of Parliament who had to leave his home in Stans near Lucerne with his whole family in 1860 in order to get some peace. During the First World War in a house in Grosserlach, also in the Mainhardt area, pots and pans flew about until the house was locked up and left empty.

In recent years there was a remarkable case in Zell near Kufstein. The police were called in. They surrounded the house and two of them, armed with flashlamps, occupied the room in which the three Fleischhacker children were sleeping. Although the house was searched and the children questioned, nothing was found. But at night suspicious noises were heard and the police took photographs. They showed stones as big as a fist flying through the air while the children slept peacefully. These stones were actually found afterwards.

Sceptics may find ground for their scepticism in the fact that in most cases of haunting, nothing unusual was found by intelligent observers. In some cases people of unsound mind were used, or children who were merely playing monkey tricks.

Still more unbelievable are the reports of so-called *apports*. A brooch disappears out of one room and suddenly materialises in another, apparently out of thin air. Before attempting an explanation, it should be pointed out that this form of manifestation is confined either to one place or to one person. In the first case it is often an old building or shed in which some strange event has taken place—a suicide, the murder of a child or some crime which arouses curiosity, fear or horror. In the second case it is mostly children in the state of puberty or people deranged in body or mind who are involved.

This leads us to accept the view of experts like Professor Bender of Freiburg University, who says that this is not a matter of spirits from the dead or revelations from another world, but rather a new problem posed by the vague and complicated nature of the soul, the problem of the split personality or hysterical disintegration. This becomes clear if we accept as *normal* a person with an integrated personality and as abnormal one who has subsidiary personalities which operate near his body and can produce certain physical effects. Because of the unstable nature of his character nothing sensible or important arises from these effects, but only what is known as spirit possession.

Poltergeists are not separate entities. They are emanations from young children. When the children are sent to an institution, the manifestations stop.

The explanation of the first case is that in the room where the emotional experience has taken place, a certain amount of the nervous energy expended remains over. As we say, "There is something in the air". Sensitive people can feel it and this excess of lingering emotion expresses itself in muffled knockings and loud noises.

Animals as well as human beings have this sensitivity, or, as we have seen in an earlier chapter, this gift of telepathy. There is a credible report of a horse that was hauling timber. It suddenly shied at a spot where one woodcutter had killed another out of jealousy. It is not surprising that such stories are heard of less and less now. Tractors do not shy and tanks roll unconcernedly over corpses.

Every story of this kind can be explained as an example of schizophrenia. But granting they are not all deception and imagination, how can one explain the action of the mind on the body?

Philosophers and psychologists have frequently pointed out that even so simple an act as raising an arm presents us with a mystery. We still do not know how the mind acts on the body or vice versa, however explainable a single reaction may be. Kant thought the problem insoluble. He did not see how a non-material entity could exist in a material body and work through it.

Table-rapping seems to me to be based on simpler conceptions. Since the nineteenth century this more or less serious society game, like the calling up of spirits, has enjoyed an ever-widening popularity. There are fashions, even in occultism. The players sit round a table and lay their hands on it so that they touch and form a continuous chain. The table soon begins to lift and rap on the floor with one or other of its legs. I have made a good number of experiments and come to the following conclusions:

1. Small round tables are best. Heavy square oak ones scarcely move at all.

2. The experiment depended very largely on the ability of the participants to concentrate. Inattentive partners or giggling girls broke the spell.

3. All the participants were expected to think of one definite movement, e.g. the table must lift on the side nearest the window, or it must rotate clockwise.

4. Often after a lapse of two to five minutes a peculiar creaking started in the wood. It was not audible when the table was standing still. The table only began to move after the creaking occurred.

5. The readiness of those taking part to believe in what they were doing played a key role. If I explained, by way of introduction, that it was all imagination, nothing happened. If I was enthusiastic and recounted former successes, the experiments went better. Many participants said they felt an itching or pain in their arms. When the experiment was over, some felt a blow on the arm.

6. What I observed with most participants was that they made unconscious muscle movements in the desired direction. The pushing and pressure naturally increases when there are four or six taking part. It can therefore be assumed that most of the movements of the table are caused by mechanical means, or, as the sceptics would say maliciously "The wiser man gives way." Obviously for these experiments in telekinesis the table is used because it is easy to handle. Why does one hear so little about boxes, books or apples moving about mysteriously?

7. What makes me still uncertain is that such naturally rational

and critical people as students can make a light table revolve at high speed. On two or three occasions I saw a rectangular table about five feet long and correspondingly wide move quickly across the room and bang against the door with only two people working it. I was one and the other was a middle-aged woman with psychic gifts. Was there not some unknown power, some kind of magnetism or odic force at work here? There have been other reports, from serious experimenters, of tables moving *without being touched,* or showing extraordinary violence, as in the case of Mrs. Silbert, a medium in Graz, who submitted to examination by R. Tischner.

8. I further noticed that when moved by ordinary mechanical means the table gave out different sounds from when the movement was inexplicable. In the latter case the table seemed lighter and moved without effort over uneven places in the carpet or floor.

9. I could never get any evidence of a spirit world. When the table was asked to give a number of raps according to an agreed schedule, it was obvious that the participants were supplying the answers. Both questions and answers were only reflecting their unconscious desires and their level of intelligence.

On the whole it is best to reserve judgment. This also applies to many of the reports from parapsychologists who claim to have heard the mysterious ringing of bells or seen a typewriter start writing without being touched. Much less has been heard of such things in the last twenty or thirty years. As we have already said, the halcyon days of the great mediums have gone.

Reports of the famous Italian woman medium, Eusapia Palladino, who died in 1918, sound almost too improbable, though they were supported by such world renowned scholars as Cesare Lombroso, Henri Bergson and Freiherr von Schrenck-Notzing.

For the sake of completeness, I will add what Peter Ringger says in his excellent publication, *New Science,* about the English physicist and parapsychologist Sir Oliver Lodge and what the latter considered to be demonstrably true from seances which he held in a bright light and under conditions of strict control.

1. A chair some distance away moved without being touched or the possibility of mechanical propulsion.

2. Clear and continued billowing of a curtain which swayed when the window was shut and no mechanical means were used.

3. A musical box winding itself up and moving about without being touched.

4. Notes played on an untouched piano.

5. A key turning in the lock, landing on the table during a seance and then returning to the lock of its own accord.

6. Audible movements and slow falling over of a table not in the circle.

These would indeed indicate remarkable powers of the human spirit and would be contrary to all materialistic thinking if there were no grounds for doubt. Even the noted Italian medium, Eusapia Palladino, has been proved a cheat. Such a fine expert as Dr. A von Schrenck-Notzing had to admit that he was taken in more than once by conjuring tricks.

Levitation

Our much appealed-to common sense warns us to be equally cautious about accepting the evidence for levitation. Objects, and even people are said to have raised themselves from the ground without using any of the technical means known to us and in spite of the pull of gravity.

Such things were known about centuries ago. Peter of Alcantara (1499-1562) and Saint Theresa of Avila (1515-1582), the foundress of the Carmelite Order, are said to have risen from the ground on many occasions in the ecstacy of prayer. In Italy the monk Joseph of Copertino (1603-1663), was beatified because he had often been seen hovering above the altar of his church and had even been able to lift others up as well. No less a person than Justinus Kerner, in his account of Friederike Hauffe, the visionary of Prevorst, recounts a similar phenomenon occurring as late as the nineteenth century. "Whenever they tried to take her to the bath, if she was in this magnetic state a strange phenomenon occurred. All her limbs and even her whole body began to twitch involuntarily. She jumped out of the water again and again as if drawn by elastic. Her attendants made every effort to keep her in the bath but her magnetic power was too strong for them and kept pushing her up. Even if she had been thrown into a river she would have floated as easily as a wooden shoe."

In former times such tests were used to try witches. Without anticipating what will be said later from the point of view of Christianity, we may point out here that whether these things are true or not, such faculties of the spirit do not go beyond the bounds of this world. Those who no longer believe in the medieval idea of a heaven above and a hell below will agree that rising in the air does not bring anyone nearer to God. Levitation can bring someone nearer to the sky, the realm of this world, but not nearer to heaven, the unreachable realm of God. As long as we are "in the body" this realm is revealed not to the physical eye but to those who dare to believe. These remarkable happenings are at most signs for which a natural explanation can be found. They can never be used as a proof of the divine kingdom to come.

One of the reasons why we cannot dismiss these things as mere deception is that in the whole course of their history, every tribe and nation has similar stories. There must at least be "something in it", even though the explanations differ. This is particularly true of so-called materialisations.

Materialisations

The well-known story of Belshazzar's feast in the Old Testament is one example. The words *mene, mene, tekel, upharsin* ("Thou art weighed in the balance and found wanting"), appeared mysteriously on the wall. Furthermore, the frightened and unhappy king also saw a ghostly hand. Was it a message from heaven or evidence of a spirit from the dead? If the latter, one would have to admit that the dead could communicate thoughts and new knowledge to the living. Or was it only a projection of the king's fears about the political situation which was already showing signs that the rule was coming to an end? A look at folklore and the results of modern research will help to clarify the answers to these questions.

Ghosts, it is claimed, appear in the dark or at midnight. They are life-size, grey or white in colour and hover in the air as though they had no weight. They are often transparent or throw no shadow. They do not stay long and vanish suddenly. Some are unrecognisable, others remind us of a familiar person by their bearing, their features, their clothing or a characteristic gesture. The "white lady" has appeared in many places and at many times, mostly in such romantic places as old castles. There is the famous white lady of Hohenzollern castle or Bernstein castle to the south of Vienna. Such ghosts appear from generation to generation and usually forebode misfortune, fire or death.

The persistence of these phenomena would seem to contradict the animistic explanation which claims that they are the projections of anxiety states of mind or the operation of mysterious energy left behind by someone who has died. The spiritists claim that the explanation would be much simpler if they were accepted as evidence that the dead reappear.

Here I must report the laboratory experiments that support

the animistic theory. Apparitions of this kind have appeared in the presence of famous mediums and are obviously not emanating from them. The founder of astro-physics, Professor Zöllner of Leipzig, carried out a number of experiments on the American medium Henry Slade, who died in 1909. Fingers, hands or arms appeared quite distinctly in his immediate neighbourhood. On one occasion Zöllner saw a non-material hand emerging from under the edge of the table and watched it for at least two minutes. Its colour was pale olive-green. Suddenly the hand reached up like lightning and held Zöllner's left arm for a whole minute. When it had disappeared, his right hand, which was under the table, was pinched so hard that he gave a shout.

The best known experiments are those which Freiherr von Schrenck-Notzing made over a number of years. I was present when he reported on his successes with the two brothers Rudi and Willi Schneider. The medium was tied hand and foot and the light was usually dimmed, though luminous strips were attached to his body. Some time after he had fallen into a trance, astonishing things began to happen. From his face, neck and shoulder poured a greyish or whitish substance which hovered and then moved slowly away. At certain spots it thickened into shapes resembling a human body. At the time telekinetic phenomena were noticed, photographs were taken and the medium's weight was measured. Within a few minutes he lost two to three ounces, and sometimes it was as much as several pounds. The mediums were always very exhausted after the seance, as though they had been working very hard. The emanation, known as ectoplasm, quickly vanished without trace, so that Schrenck-Notzing was not able to confirm former chemical analyses of the substance, though he claims to have found cells of epithelium and things of that kind. They come from the medium's body, not from the ectoplasm.

There is no value in the plaster casts of supposed spirit hands. The famous conjuror and contortionist, Houdini, had no difficulty in producing similar ones. Some experimenters, like the engineer F. Grunewald, claim to have noticed a change in the ionisation of the surrounding air while the ectoplasm was present. Others felt a breath of cold air such as was mentioned earlier in connection with spontaneous apparitions.

If there is any truth in all this, many spirit appearances could be explained as materialisations. Unknown mediums would then be giving off ectoplasm which would hover in the room for a time and be seen by this person or that. The unsatisfactory thing about this is that materialisations are no longer common today. Parapsychologist institutes confine themselves entirely to cases of clairvoyance and precognition. Were the others only due to mental disease or hysteria?

This question arises when you look at the famous photograph of Conan Doyle. This writer of crime stories, who made himself rich and famous with his master detective, Sherlock Holmes, was also a convinced spiritist. He promised to appear to his friends after his death if it was at all possible. For several months nothing happened. Then at one of the seances held by the Society for Psychical Research something unusual occurred. Independently of the medium, some ectoplasm appeared about a foot and a half above him in the form of three heads, the middle one of which was immediately recognised as Conan Doyle's. But paper is passive and it is easy to fix up photos. Was this truth or pious deception?

The South American medium, Carlos Mirabelli, practised brazen deception. His materialisations were said to become persons of flesh and blood. Two doctors were supposed to have examined them for a quarter of an hour for blood pressure, heart beat and breathing, after which the wraiths disappeared into thin air. These reports were invalidated because Mirabelli became the dictatorial leader of a sect and would not allow any checking by unbelievers. There are therefore no scientifically incontestable reports on his skill.

The revered professor Karl Heim was enthusiastic in his belief that Mirabelli had given the death blow to materialism; that the facts made nonsense of attempts to explain the world by theories of determinism or mechanism. Unfortunately this view cannot be substantiated.

When occultists point out that modern physics can change matter into energy and vice versa, they are not making a sound comparison. Where experiments do produce such changes it is only on the tiniest scale in micro-physics. In the realm of macro-physics, hitherto valid laws of nature and causality still obtain. If Mirabelli's statements were correct many natural laws would have to be defined differently, and their sphere of operation as well. Fortunately for us, the world is not a chaos of magic, but a physical realm which is divinely ordered. The same would be true if the anthroposophists were right in talking about an ether body, a kind of spiritual matter. I do not wish here to impugn the genuineness of Rudolf Steiner. His *Knowledge of Higher Worlds* remains his private possession; there is nothing to prove him right or wrong. It is a matter of belief, not knowledge. In these circumstances people who wish to acquire this "knowledge" must accept nothing less than a blind, authoritarian belief.

Reincarnations and Soul Transference

Rudolf Steiner knew the religions of India intimately. It is in them that we meet with the age-old belief in reincarnation. The popular word for it is transmigration of souls. Karl Hutten prefers the word reventism. According to this belief we have hundreds of other lives besides the one on this earth. Buddha claimed having passed through one million eight hundred thousand births before becoming the Enlightened One. The soul must put on one form after another until through its good deeds, its *Karma*, its life becomes so ennobled that it attains Nirvana, union with the whole, and so ends the painful cycle.

The Bible gives various reasons for believing that we have only one life on earth. It proclaims God as the Creator and Lover of a world which it does not, like the Indians, regard only as an illusion (Maya). The body is therefore no mere shell, but has a closely knit unity with the soul. Therefore the present life is a gift from God and of the highest importance. "It is appointed unto men once to die, but after this the judgment." (Heb. 9:27.)

But let us make a sober enquiry into the facts. Are there any proofs that man remembers a former life? If there were such proofs, we should be taken far beyond all the phenomena we have been discussing, for these only have to do with an extension of the present life. As we are concerned with facts and proof, the conceptions of great poets are worth our consideration, though they are not decisive. One thinks of Goethe writing to Frau von Stein. "Alas, thou wast in far off times my sister or my wife."

In his story of the Bead Game, Hermann Hesse makes the boys of a provincial academy write an essay on their former life in times long past. Experiences of "having seen it before" are of this nature. People get a sudden feeling that they have seen a certain town or scene before. But such experiences are only vague, and besides, they are often due to a purely mental process or a lack of co-ordination between the lobes of the brain cortex that are concerned with the remembering process. It has even been possible with the aid of electrical stimuli to produce an artificial impression of recollecting something like a landscape.

Our enquiries here, as everywhere else, show that a large number of the reports on recollection, even those with a definite content, contain some deception. A few offer unsolved riddles.

The visionary of Geneva was exposed by a psychologist named Flournoy. She thought she was the incarnation of the daughter of an Arab Sheik. She actually wrote a row of Arabic signs in a trance, but from left to right instead of the other way round! It turned out that she had seen these signs in a dedication an author had put at the beginning of his book of travels. This shows how our subconscious memory preserves countless impressions which normal people entirely forget, but which may crop up at any time. They offer however, no proof of a former existence. The famous Aramaic sentences from the time of Christ recited by Theresa Neumann may have had the same cause. It was discovered that her sister had worked for a professor of ancient oriental languages.

An equally simple explanation was found in the case of Bridey Murphy, which created such a stir in America a few years ago. A woman named Virginia Tighe, born in 1923 and living in Pueblo, Colorado, was sent into a deep sleep several times by the hypnotist, Morey Bernstein. She made statements about a former life she had lived in Ireland as Bridey Murphy. Her description of circumstances, places, folk dances and so on were so accurate that they started a craze in America for occult experiences. Thousands allowed themselves to be hypnotised and discovered that they had been kings of Egypt or sailors under Columbus! In Houston, Texas, one medium began to neigh like a horse and said he had been a horse in his former life!

Pastor Wally White of Chicago produced an explanation that had escaped both reporters and psychologists. Virginia Tighe had known an Irish family when she was quite small. The mother's maiden name was Bridey Murphy, and she had told her children all kinds of things about Ireland. All these things had emerged from Virginia's subconscious when she was hypnotised.

The astonishing case of Kumari Shanti Devi, an Indian girl born in 1926, still awaits an explanation. The events happened about 1936. She was living in Delhi and said she had already been born once in 1902 and had lived in Muttra, 120 kilometres away. She was married to a draper named Chaubey and after giving birth to a son, she had died. As she kept on talking about this, her family made enquiries to find out whether such a person as Chaubey really existed in Muttra. Shanti was nine at the time. A letter from Chaubey confirmed what the girl had said. He also sent a relative and later came himself. Shanti recognised both at once. After they had ascertained that the girl had never been outside Delhi, a committee was formed to act as witnesses while the girl was on a planned visit to Muttra to see whether she would recognise any people or places. At the railway station Shanti recognised another relative of Chaubey in a large crowd. She was then put in a carriage and left to say where she wanted to be driven. The driver was to follow all her directions. She directed him to the part of the town where Chaubey lived and recognised the house although it had recently been painted in different colours. She also went to the home of her former parents whom she singled out from fifty other people and gave their correct names.

It is difficult to explain a case of such exact precision by clairvoyance or by the tapping of the collective unconscious, what the Indians call the "Akascha Chronicle". These reports would have to be tested more closely by unprejudiced western psychologists. The average Indian has a vivid imagination, as in the case of the Sadhu Sundar Singh. The question arises too why there are millions of people, many of them highly strung and sensitive, who never have such knowledge or experiences. Why do we hear of only rare cases, many of which do not stand up to investigation? The same question may be asked of the so-called bilocations or journeys of the soul. In 1947 an Italian monk named Father Pio is said to have appeared to someone suffering from heart disease in Cosenza in the southern part of Italy, while he himself remained in his monastery near Rome. The following morning a wonderful scent of violets filled the patient's room. This raises a problem of faith. What do the sick do who do not know any miracle worker, or have neither the money nor the courage to send him a telegram? Would they not be at such a disadvantage as to make one doubt the justice of God?

Professor Ernesto Bozzano of Italy has reported a number of similar cases in primitive Congo tribes told him by missionaries. Any form of scientific check however is impossible. How much is real and how much is imagination?

Apparitions

We ended the last section with a question. The following stories of apparitions are not altogether without possibility of proof, but they also raise questions and doubts.

I was called one evening to a young man who was in a very disturbed state. He was a relief lorry driver and had been driving on his usual route. In the forest of Mainhardt he had to stop and get out in the dark. He had not gone many paces when he was overwhelmed with a feeling of fear. He stopped rooted to the spot as he saw a large black form coming towards him. This alarming apparition came right up to him and passed through him. He let out a yell and rushed back to the lorry shouting, "Give it gas! Give it gas!" I had to talk to him for a long time, pray with him and give him a sleeping draught before he would calm down. He was an ordinary young man, full of vitality and a non-churchgoer. Nothing like this has happened to him before or since. In course of time he became more serious-minded, attended church, and took the sacrament. His mother was alarmed at first but later rejoiced at his development. He had not been drinking the night the apparition occurred, but from then on he avoided as far as possible driving through those woods in the dark.

Another example was told me by a family living in Stuttgart. After a long illness, the father had died at eight o'clock in the evening and was lying in his coffin on the ground floor. Exhausted with nursing him for so long, his wife was sleeping with her daughter on the first floor. On the second floor there was a workshop where he had often spent his time when he was well. At two o'clock in the morning, his daughter was awakened by a familiar sound. She heard her father's footsteps as they went up to the workshop and the door shut in the usual way. While she was listening, her mother woke up and also heard the footsteps moving overhead. "Father!" she exclaimed.

The former of these two examples is the more puzzling, because the young man was completely unsuspecting and had gone through no emotional excitement. Of the second case it might be said that it was not a post mortem appearance as we tried to point out in a former chapter on telepathy and clairvoyance. But it raises the question whether the dead man really did return. When does death actually set in? Is it not often such a gentle passing that there is no clear dividing line between life and death? Is not an easier explanation that people who are emotionally upset often indulge in projection; that they only see and hear in their imagination?—in this case a beloved father going as usual to his room? This does not mean that every occurrence can be explained in this way.

Let us take a third example, which Fanny Moser cites in her book on the subject of haunting.

A Swiss married couple were taking a walk in the meadows on Gilieila, a mountain near Seewis 4,900 feet high. Suddenly the husband, who didn't live in that part, saw an old man in peasant dress disappear through the locked door of a barn. He immediately told his wife who had lagged a bit behind. She said that people round there knew of this apparition. It was a former owner of the meadow who was said to have been very avaricious. The husband's description of his appearance and dress accorded perfectly with what the local peasants and miners said.

As it happened I was able to investigate this story of Fanny Moser's, for I knew the couple well. The woman is strong-minded and sensible; the husband was a successful business man, and had a high regard for the truth. He has never had such an experience since, though that one was years ago. Before he died he gave me another exact description of the old man "on his word of honour".

It is said by some parapsychologists (as by some researchers in other fields) that the simplest theory is the best. But which is the simplest? Is it the spiritist one which claims that the dead can exercise power over the living, or is it the animistic one which would say of this case that the legend of Gilieila existed in the subconscious mind of the wife, who came from the neighbourhood? When she got to the spot she transferred the image to her husband some 150 yards in front and this stimulated his eyesight so that he thought he saw it. Or was there that "something in the air" we talked of earlier, some energy left over from a former inhabitant? Leading parapsychologists admit that there is not yet any clear explanation.

Helen Christaller, authoress and wife of a parson, records having seen a man's white head float through the bedroom. It turned out later that a young man had been shot or had committed suicide in the house. C. G. Jung relates how in a haunted house in England, he became aware of an unbearable odour which reminded him of a case in his clinic of an old woman with an open cancer sore. A few nights later as he was lying in bed he heard rustlings, knockings and a crackling noise, while from outside there came bangs on the wall. It was a moonlight night and there was no wind. He felt something near him. With some difficulty he opened his eyes and saw on the pillow beside him the head of an old woman with her right eye wide open staring at him. The left half of the face below the eye was missing. It was so sudden and unexpected that he sprang out of bed, lit a candle and spent the rest of the night in an armchair. The next day he moved into another room where he slept well two weekends running without the least disturbance.

Professor Jung's view is that there must have been traces of an odour left behind by former occupiers of the room which had stimulated his subconscious mind and produced a pictorial memory of the old woman suffering from cancer. As no one knew who the previous occupants of the house were, it was not possible

72

to carry out further enquiries. So we still face the dilemma of having to choose between the mutually hostile animistic and spiritualistic explanations.

The Visionary of Prevorst

In the foregoing section we have spoken of ghosts who appear but do not speak. It would provide the best proof of their reality if they did, especially if what they said could not have been known to any living person. Today spirits appear to speak through the mouth of a medium, but there are cases where a direct voice is heard while the medium is talking of something else. These so-called *cross-correspondences* have produced some remarkable results in this respect. These results are confirmed by various mediums operating in different seances, but what is said is so petty and unimportant that this has been regarded as a mere game for cultured people who have nothing better to do.

Some reports are so drawn up as to make one think that a living person has penetrated the curtain of death, or rather that the folds of this curtain have moved mysteriously to allow a glimpse of another world to be caught. The story of the visionary of Prevorst deserves special mention in this respect.

Friederike Hauffe (1801-1829), *née* Wanner, came from the village of Prevorst high up in the Mainhadt Forest. Her grandfather, living in Löwenstein, had second sight and she early showed signs of possessing the same gift. She married at the age of twenty and soon after had a nervous breakdown which caused her to become helpless and bed-ridden. In 1826, she was taken to Weinsberg to be treated by the senior medical officer, Dr. Justinus Kerner. She remained there till shortly before her death which took place in Löwenstein. The gilded cross over her grave can be seen far down the valley. It was the gift of a count out of gratitude for the cure of his wife's protracted mental illness which Friederike had been able to effect after eight days of prayer. Kerner and others who knew her, say that she was devout, pure and loving. She never received any money or advantage from her pronouncements. She implored God, sometimes in simple verse, to free her from the gift of second sight. Justinus Kerner was himself a poet and very romantic. There may, therefore, have been some affinity between him and his patient which heightened, if it did not provoke, her visions. However that may be, he also worked on a scientific basis. By his use of sebacic acid he became one of the pioneers of modern psychological tests. Joachim Bodamer's latest edition of Kerner's book on Friederike shows the doctor to have been a keen and accurate observer.

The first event at Weinsberg recorded by Kerner is highly typical. After only a few days of treatment, she was disturbed by a spirit. She gave an exact description of it and it corresponded with that of an accountant who had died several years before. Kerner recognised the person at once. She said he was telling her about some large embezzlements by which he had cheated his firm. The proof was to be found in a file in the room of a particular house nearby which she described accurately. They were on page eighty, beginning at the letter "J". Kerner was sceptical at first, but decided to investigate. He and a magistrate named Heyd found this page in a book shelf at the magistrates' court. At the urgent pleading of the spirit, an agreement was reached with the firm. The judge himself drew up a report which stated that the hitherto unnoticed embezzlements of the accountant had amounted over the years to some twenty thousand guilders. Kerner relates that when they came across this sheet that had lain unnoticed under piles of others for six years, a shiver had gone down their spines.

He rules out telepathy here because no one knew of the crime or had any interest in uncovering it. He was doubtful too about its being clairvoyance. How could such a thing occur to her? The house whose basement the man had occupied was, it is true, not far away and the explanation might be that the dead man sent out an impulse which normal people would not perceive, but which would penetrate the sensitive spirit of the sick woman.

To end this section, here is a pleasant example. Christoph Blumhardt told it to a large assembly of mourners at his father's graveside on February 28th, 1880. It concerns a hymn his father had made up beginning, "Jesus is the Victor Who all His foes o'ercomes." The son said that a number of people from Möttlingen were returning with his father from a missionary gathering in the neighbouring village of Ostelsheim in 1844 on the Feast of the Apostles. As they were going through the wood his father made up these verses which he immediately recited to his companions. The men sang them lustily to the tune "Great God, we praise Thee". They could hardly believe their ears when they heard that they were not alone in their singing. The hymn had been taken up by an invisible choir. It seemed as if a host from heaven had descended to join in. Full of astonished joy they hurried home and there another miracle awaited them. A woman named Gottliebin Dittus met his father at the door and recited the same hymn. It seemed as if the invisible singers had preceded his father and told the woman about the hymn.

Conclusions

What has Christianity to say to all this? We have first to accept
the findings of science. But these, as we have seen, are not yet
clear. There is neither a satisfactory explanation nor a united
opinion. While Driesch and Mattiesen firmly believe the dead
can communicate with us, equally famous scholars like Tischner
and Dessoir do not.

It would be a complete misunderstanding of the Christian faith
if Christians ranged themselves on one side or the other. It is
unimportant for the faith whether the dead do get in touch with
us or not. What we see and hear in this world belongs to this
world only, though it may open up new horizons for us. Even the
cosmonauts remain limited to this world. We are all bounded by
it and ought not to try to cross the frontier of death. Even such
a strong opponent of intellectualism as the theologian Adolf
Köberle, referring to the parable of the rich man and Lazarus
(Luke 16: 19 ff.), says it does not open a gateway into eternity.
In the parable the rich man is shown the right way to get into
touch with God. The living "have Moses and the prophets; let
them listen to them". And the sending of angels was refused.
"If they will not hear Moses and the prophets, they will not believe though one rise from the dead" (Luke 16: 31). Only belief
in the resurrection of our Lord can assure us of our own resurrection and eternal life, not the doubtful appearance of any spirits,
who do not seem to be wiser than we are or know more than we do.

As we are not supposed to look behind the iron curtain of death,
so we should not seek to know the future by occult means. "The
wages of sin is death", said the Apostle (Rom. 6: 23). People
who try to explore the realm of the dead are running away from
the fact that death is the inevitable lot of man.

The scientist can, and is clearly called to, explore this world
in which we live, so that having explored it we can enjoy it, but to
explore the regions beyond the grave (and to do it by occult powers)
is surely wrong.

It may be objected that in rare cases like the visionary of
Prevorst or Blumhardt's hymn, God has granted a glimpse into
His supernatural kingdom. I would reply that even if we lived
on ten, twenty or a hundred years after death, it would only be a
prolongation of the present world and by no means a proof of
the other. "Eye hath not seen, ear hath not heard, nor hath it

entered into the heart of man what God hath prepared for them that love Him" (1 Cor. 2: 9). Such phenomena as we have been discussing do indeed contradict the extreme materialists' claim that everything ends with the decomposition of the body, but they give no evidence of God's promises of the forgiveness of sins and a life of everlasting bliss which we find in the Bible.

What was granted to Friederike Hauffe, J. C. Blumhardt and Friedrich Oetinger, who is reported to have preached to the dead, is exceptional. It was a mysterious and divine gift imparted to a select few. There is a report of one of our greatest and most devout preachers, Johann Friedrich Oberlin of Steintal, that his faithful wife and counsellor returned to give him help and advice for years after her death. It is not to be supposed that such a practical social reformer who helped the poor in a thousand ways would be the victim of purely subjective imagination. These gifts are not given to every man and no one should attempt to acquire them.

What are we to think then of the stories in the Bible? In 1 Samuel 28, we read how King Saul went secretly to the witch of Endor. Accustomed as she was to practise all kinds of deception, she was alarmed when Samuel, the dead judge, actually appeared and talked with the king. Matthew records that at the death of Jesus, "the earth did quake, the rocks rent and the graves were opened and many bodies of saints which slept arose and came out of the graves after His resurrection and went into the Holy City and appeared unto many" (Matt. 27: 52 f.).

These two examples confirm what we have said above. It is true they show a belief in a realm of the dead and in a kind of intermediary stage, but this is far from the final hope of transfiguration offered to believers. The story of Saul is meant to be a warning. He had once driven fortune-tellers, soothsayers and mediums out of the country. The spells of the witch of Endor were as wicked and godless as the king's desire to force God to tell him the future. That is why God withdrew His favour and Saul finally committed suicide on the field of battle (cf. Deut. 18: 9-12; Isa. 8: 19).

As regards the dead who appeared to the faithful at Easter, we never hear of them again. They never reappear and the early Christians never consulted them. It was therefore a unique and isolated apparition which can only be explained in connection with Christ bursting the bonds of death.

Christ's appearances to the disciples after the crucifixion are not on the same plane with the appearances of any other people who were dead. God was revealing Himself to the Apostles in the form of the living Lord so that they might believe that He whom men had abased and persecuted was in reality the Exalted One of God.

The gentle but manifest reproof the risen Jesus gave to Thomas, "Blessed are they who have not seen but yet have believed", applies to us all. (John 20: 29). The real believers who see visions concur in this. In spite of all her remarkable psychic experiences, the visionary of Prevorst said, "A belief in spirits has nothing to do with religious belief. Man does not need it in order to please God, so the Scriptures have little to say about it." When a visitor asked Oberlin about his apparitions, he replied, "The Gospel is enough for me. I should not like to waste time on extraordinary and even dangerous matters when it could be more usefully employed both for others and myself."

Ghosts, hauntings and spiritism, then, are no subjects for the true believer, but rather for the research scientist.

Is then the connection between the living and the dead entirely broken off? Must we, by a determined act of faith, abandon the dead to the invisible world without our being able to do anything for them? No, that is not it. The Church is our great home for the very reason that it includes the living and the dead. We both await our salvation and the coming of God's new world. Because Christ is the Head of the Church, through Him we enjoy a bond of unity with those who are "fallen asleep" (Heb. 12: 1, 22-24).

6

Spiritual Healing

Therapeutics

IN 1930, Stefan Zweig published his book *Healing through the Spirit* which contains a fascinating account of the nature and development of the art of healing. He describes primitive man's world of magic in which everything was endowed with mysterious powers that threatened him from all sides. Even sickness was regarded as an enemy who wanted to destroy him. So he sought the help of the tribal chief who, as both priest and doctor, could get into touch with these hidden powers. Every culture begins with a religion and every healing process with exorcism. The struggle for health was not therefore a struggle against a particular disease, but a wrestling with God. Medicine began with a theology, a cult, a ritual and magic. Its aim was to stiffen man's resistance to a divine testing.

Some two thousand five hundred years ago, the Greek philosophers introduced objective thought, and there was a revival of it in the eighteenth century, the Age of Enlightenment, when men began to find out the inner workings of the body. This was essential for effecting real cures of diseases and also for uncovering the secrets of nature. Here are some of the findings of the time. The art of healing, formerly the calling of a few mysteriously gifted persons, becomes a craft. It becomes objective and professional. Technicalities, apparatus, organisation and specialisation become paramount. The sick person is *treated*. He becomes the object. That he has to co-operate with the efforts of the doctor is no longer taken for granted. Drugs, chemicals and other material remedies triumph. The surgeon becomes the uncrowned king.

This was followed by a silent swing of the pendulum, as so often happens in life. Powers of the unconscious mind were discovered, chiefly by the pioneers of the fruitful romantic movement. Their influence has lasted down to the present time. Exceptional geniuses led the way as they have done all through history. At first material and mechanical means were not rejected out of hand. About 1775, a Viennese Jesuit, Father Max Hell, thought he had found healing power in magnets which he fastened to various parts of the patient's body. Franz Anton Mesmer (1734-1815), made the brilliant discovery that his patients felt relief when he stroked the injured part rhythmically; the aid of magnets was not at all necessary. But he reverted later on to the use of healing water and gave public demonstrations. In place of electrical magnetism he had used animal magnetism which he claimed flowed evenly through every healthy body. His demonstrations soon became fashionable at the courts of Paris and Vienna. Often they were the scene of mass hysteria. Women laughed, wept, shrieked, went into ecstasies or fainted.

The ideas and methods of the American healer, Phineas Parkhurst Quimby (1802-1866), are of decisive importance. After many experiments in hypnosis he became convinced that not only hypnotised people, but people leading ordinary lives were living in a world of illusion which prevented them from recognising reality. A new way of thinking was needed. Hence the name *New Thought* given later to his movement. Its protagonists claim that this new thought creates a reality that is good, harmonious and perfect. They consider all evil and sickness as fundamental illusion. Just as a man under hypnosis can *think away* his pain, so can anyone in the waking state. By regarding the pain and its causes as illusion you make them disappear.

The German branch of the *New Thought Alliance* publishes a monthly paper called the *White Flag*. The Alliance not only claims to heal through the mind, but promises, as a logical consequence, to overcome the ills of old age and finally free people from death. All these ills, it claims, are due to a wrong way of thinking which is, unfortunately, to be found in the Bible as well. For more than three thousand years Psalm ninety, verse ten, has been preached as law and the last chapter of the Book of the Wisdom of Solomon, with its wonderful description of man's decline in old age, has been held up to us, if not as a model, at least with the suggestion that such an end is unavoidable. Such negative ideas are grounds enough for getting resigned to growing old.

One of the important patients treated by Mr. Quimby was a lady named Mary Baker Eddy. According to some reports Mrs. Eddy was a bundle of suffering who for years had endured cramps, paralysis, and pains in the back. In 1866 she attained complete recovery after reading a New Testament account of Jesus' healing power. Mrs. Eddy became the founder and leader of the religious movement called Christian Science. Thousands of practitioners heal through her influence. Her ideas are used as the basis of prayer. Her *Science and Health* is read in Christian Science churches. This is not the place to go more deeply into this movement. In our opinion it has now become a sect and it should be studied as such.

But in Christian Science there is a grain of real truth. For this reason genuine scientists have made a serious study of it.

Freud plumbed the depths of the mind and healed nervous diseases without medicine, shock treatment or force. His over-emphasis of the sex motive, which threatened to disintegrate the personality, has been corrected by some of his followers. Men like Jung, Pfister, Pfahler, Fritz Künkel and Victor von Weizsäcker, who was in charge of the psychosomatic clinic in Heidelberg, became the founders of psychotherapy. They have studied whole com-plexes of diseases which have a mental as well as a physical com-ponent. The one works on the other and together they form a tangled syndrome, a confluence of different diseases. In this con-nection they mention stomach and bowel troubles, asthma, bad circulation, heart trouble, even diabetes, tuberculosis of the lung and allergies as being among these complexes.

Victor von Weizsäcker describes the case of a landlord who went to law with his neighbour over a field. After prolonged litigation he failed to get justice. A sense of grievance weighed on his mind and "hit", as we rightly say, the stomach. This led on to gall bladder trouble. Once the pain and inflammation thus caused have led to an organic derangement, the surgeon is the only hope, though an operation does not cure the real trouble. At an earlier stage the advice and guidance of an understanding psychologist would have healed him.

Of course, all these doctors value the help of religion very highly. They consider the confession and penitence inspired by a sympathetic parson as most useful.

Fifty years ago there was a complaint about too much selling of medicines. Today the layman is inclined to go to the other extreme when he hears Weizsäcker assert that the patient is him-self the cause of his illness, or when Freud says than an accident on the road was caused by the victim's unconscious mind, be-cause he wanted to punish himself, or when he is told that his organs "welcome", as Freud says, the microbes of an infectious disease in the air.

Friedrich Schiller had a deep understanding of the human heart. As a young man, he gave a dissertation in 1780 in which he gave an example of a decline in physical strength because of homesickness. He also made the important discovery that the cold shivers of a feverish patient are the same as those of a wrong-doer when he realises his guilt.

In this connection it is good to know that in many countries joint committees of doctors and ministers have been formed and that in many hospitals there is joint action. In most countries of the Western world there are groups and fellowships which teach the subject of wholeness for the body, soul and mind, thus bringing complete deliverance for those in need. Such help is effected by various means, including the laying on of hands with prayer.

Church leaders are very open to this kind of endeavour, as witness the Lambeth Conference. Experts in psychotherapy and in psychohygiene, like Professor Heinrich Meng of Basel, are keen about these problems. Psychohygiene seeks not only to cure, but also to prevent by means of sounder and more understanding education of mind and body. In this way it saves children from making mistakes or suffering from complexes and diseases.

Mental hygiene has a special part to play in the matter of superstition and superstitious people. Superstition is an expression of psychic uncertainty and shows traces of man's earliest steps in the cultivation of his mind. Most neurotics are superstitious and slaves to their neuroses. But research into the unconscious has opened the way to an understanding of many of the ideas underlying superstition and has enabled us to estimate their effect on health and sickness, destiny and death.

Signs of Degeneration

With genuine faith and true science co-operating to help the fearful and the sick to spiritual and bodily health everything would be all right but for a neurotic superstition which has recently been proclaiming successes and leading millions astray.

Modern miracle workers who go from town to town and country to country promising faith healing are well-known figures. They hold mass meetings and raise the expectations of the crowd to a high pitch with advertisements, music and witnesses who are supposed to have been cured. There is an atmosphere of tension in the room. People keep shouting Hallelujah until at last the healer approaches the sick, lined up on seats or beds in front of him. Now and again a cripple does indeed throw away his crutches and rush joyously from the hall. Someone else may shout, "I can see again!" Doubters and disbelievers are easily carried away by all this.

The worst feature of such meetings is that the occasional use of the Bible gives the impression that Jesus Christ, the true Healer, is glorified through them. The borderline between faith and super-stition is very fine here. Serious thought and God's help are needed to distinguish between the true and false prophets.

A few years ago Bruno Gröning's star rose like a meteor and then slowly petered out. He had established a headquarters in the Traberhoff Hotel, near Rosenheim. The scene was a memorable one. He was surrounded by a host of helpers and secretaries, among them a number of spongers who were only interested in the money the patients paid, often their last penny, in order to be healed. Thousands camped in the open, often in pouring rain, and waited till the miracle worker appeared on the balcony and threw down to the crowd below his silver paper balls to which he had imparted his healing power.

Many doctors did indeed agree that some powers of suggestion proceeded from him and that he gave many patients fresh courage and stimulus. But they too were the victims of suggestion. Other groups of doctors discovered that out of a thousand patients, at most two or three were genuinely cured. None of them were suffering any organic trouble. Dr. Alexander Mitscherlich of the Psychosomatic Institute in Heidelberg was devastating in his judg-ment. "Gröning is not a fit person to practise healing. He is im-petuous, uncontrolled and of a degenerate type, subject to great changes of mood and with an unhealthy desire for fame. His success is due to his powers of suggestion. There is no question of supernatural ability and no real psychotherapy about it."

I myself saw the film which his disciples made in order to spread his fame. A small boy is seen working his way laboriously forward with jerky movements and distorted features. It was the typical picture of a semi-cripple, but there was no genuine cure. Variations in health and powers of locomotion are frequent characteristics of this kind of illness. But what can you expect from a miracle healer who explained that he kept his goitre because it served as a receptacle for all the bad and poisonous diseases he drew on himself from his patients!

Any lasting cures he may have effected do not weigh in the balance against the thousands who suffered disillusionment and despair, or had a recurrence of their trouble. He only made mention of the name of Christ in passing. He had no knowledge of the Bible nor a strong faith.

Hermann Zaiss, on the other hand, who, like Gröning, died in 1958, placed his Christian faith at the centre of his work and wanted to be an evangelist with the same healing gift as the early disciples. His followers gathered round him to form a

"Community of Christians". It is one of the many branches of the world-wide pentecostal movement, and has many of the characteristics of a sect.

What I heard and saw of Brother Zaiss at a large meeting in Heilbronn-Sontheim made me feel very sad. I went with an open mind, ready to acknowledge any miracle and glad to admit that the Spirit bloweth where it listeth and that one's own church must be ready to repent for its lack of faith.

Though he quoted the Bible a good deal and gave popular biblical messages, and asserted that he, Hermann Zaiss, was nothing but a poor sinner, yet in his meetings a different spirit was clearly present. There were longer preparations, many hymns were sung and orders were given to raise hands, clap, stand up and sit down. When at last Zaiss turned to the sick people, nothing more happened than any hypnotist could have achieved in one evening with a few patients. Zaiss put his thumbs into the ears of a woman who was nearly deaf and said, "Mary, can you hear me?" She said she could and the eyes of the audience shone! No one enquired what sort of deafness it was nor how much the old woman could already hear.

A young man with jerky arm and leg movements left the hall cured. How much of a cripple was he before, and how long did his ability to walk last? An old man got on to the platform with the aid of crutches. Zaiss snatched them from him roughly and threw them away. "You do not need them any more," he said. Later I saw the poor man looking for his crutches and then hobble out of the hall with them. The looks in the eyes of those who were lying on stretchers were heartrending. Zaiss kept passing them by, only glancing at them as he did so. Was his faith failing him? or was theirs? Would not this have been a unique opportunity to pray for, and operate, a real cure to the glory of God?

I was depressed at the sight of so much misery, so many unfulfilled hopes. I am not exaggerating when I say that whole washing-baskets were being filled with ten and twenty mark notes from people of very moderate means.

I am ready to admit that Zaiss was convinced of his mission and did not want to enrich himself. Also there are many doctors who, like Dr. Kötteritz of Heilbronn, have seen their patients improve and even been cured and the cure has lasted for years. One was a woman who suffered from atrophy of the spine and tetanus. She was healed and believes that Christ did it. She is now giving devoted attention to other sick people.

In the case of those extreme American men who claim to be able to heal at will, judgment must be harsher. Their stories of successes are even more astonishing and unbelievable and their advertising more blatant. A newspaper report of February, 1956, stated that at the conclusion of a mission in Karlsruhe there were a hundred and thirty-seven testimonies to healing and more were coming in daily. When sorted, they showed that the Lord Jesus had cured, among others, the following diseases: heart failure, bad circulation, indigestion, constipation, leukaemia, cancer, colic, anaemia. It was not therefore astonishing that a missioner claimed to have healed twenty-five thousand people at one session in Durban, South Africa. One of our best experts, Dr. Kurt Koch, made a thorough investigation and came to the conclusion that this man was an "occult fanatic".

The Munich author and lawyer, Kurt Trampler, went about his healing work from a higher moral standpoint and with less publicity. He believed that he could deal psychically with patients whether they were with him or a hundred miles away. He could feel a pain in his body at the exact place where it was in the other person's and could then send out radiations which had the power of quick healing. He believed too that this power could be transferred to small aluminium sheets which then acquired curative power. He also cured animals and made beans grow better by means of this radiation.

The Freiburg Institute for Parapsychology was able to confirm his successes. After a series of tests, the general impression was that Trampler's effectiveness was mainly concerned with changes that were subjectively understandable and might, of course, have certain consequences for the patient. For example, the rheumatoid arthritis of a woman patient was from an objective point of view and according to the organic diagnosis, incurable, but her pain so far disappeared that she was able to walk quite easily. Placebo pills will also often drive away pain if the patient and, as far as possible, the doctor believes them to be a new and excellent remedy. Dr. Rehder's tests have shown clearly what Trampler's healing power consists in. Attempts to heal at a distance were fruitless if the patient knew nothing about it, but they succeeded if the patient had been told that a gifted healer would be sending rays at such and such a time the next day. This was effective even when the healer knew nothing about it and was not treating the patient. Dr. Rehder, of Hamburg, is a specialist for internal diseases. He concludes that the *content* of the healer's faith, whether religious or magical, has no effect on the success or failure. The really effective thing is his own conviction and it is doubly effective when the patient shares the same confidence, e.g. in homeopathic medicines.

In view of all this there is no need to go into other modern examples in which superstition plays a part, except perhaps, for a mention of eye diagnosis. Instead of diagnosis of general disorders from the appearance of the eye this entails the diagnosis of 72 specific malfunctions through the colour of various parts of the iris; this borders on superstition. When the eye specialists at the Tübingen clinic tested diagnoses of this kind the results were more a source of merriment to the doctors than of help to the patients. The temerity of tampering with the precious gift of health without previous training and from a fixed idea savours of sectarianism.

The ever-increasing use of pills of all kinds as medicine is another indication of superstition. Professor Arthur Jores estimates that about thirty thousand remedies are on sale in Germany alone, many of them quite worthless. Of course they may have a soothing effect on those who believe in them, but, apart from a doctor's prescription, or cases of serious illness, taking pills is a sign of anxiety and fear of ill-health which mean a lack of trust in God.

Attitude to Adopt.

After this review we are in a position to form a judgment. We will first take the findings of conscientious doctors and psychologists. They say that in these cases the sick person is not really cured.

He is taken by surprise and even done violence to. The impatience and despair of chronic invalids meets the restless and unstable person of the healer and both are excited by each other till a sudden effect is produced which later on may lead to severe mental and bodily harm. A good doctor rejects this as a kind of magic to which men pay reverence and attribute supernatural power. This is not because he is rationalist or purely materialist. He seeks rather to establish a relationship with the patient which is not only rational but understanding, a human relationship which inspires genuine confidence, one in which the invalid finds the doctor often ignorant and fallible like himself and yet doing his utmost to help. This ripening friendship between patient and doctor leads then to lasting cure or at least bearable suffering.

The purpose of psychotherapy is not to bind spells on people, as the magicians do, but to free people from the spells that bind them. Only when patient and doctor meet frankly as fellow human beings will the realisation come that illness is nearly always the consequence of a wrong relationship to the environment, a reaction to impressions and experiences that have not been rightly understood, a wrong spiritual attitude which neither medicines nor apparatus can correct.

When all these quack doctors talk of divine powers, of a higher calling, to which they lay claim, or of being in harmony with a metaphysical universe, trained doctors become sceptical and turn with disgust from the Church and its faith. It is no wonder that so honest an expert as Freud regarded all religion as an "infantile neurosis".

Matter of fact doctors have told these quacks and members of the many sects, that all their ecstasies and miracle-working lack conscientiousness and genuine love. Astonishing cures are heard of, but little is heard of the after-care of the sick, or of the frank admission that this brother or that has not been fully healed.

There will be some Christians who will not agree with this. They will say that they are aware that there are many fields in which healing will come through the human minds and along natural lines, though the workings of the soul are ultimately inexplicable. There is such a thing as the healing of the Holy Spirit through the power of God and in the name of Jesus Christ. Jesus appears in the New Testament not only as the Saviour from sin and guilt but also as Healer of the sick, as in the cases of the two blind men, Legion, the man sick of the palsy, and the lepers. A veritable springtime of health dawned in Galilee and Jerusalem! And Christ gave His powers to His disciples as well as to the early Christian communities. Are we not then diminishing the full Gospel if we leave the sick entirely to the surgeon and psychotherapist? Ought we not to pray for a revival of the gifts of the first Christians? (1 Cor. 12: 28).

These questions must be taken seriously. We all long to see a living Christian community in which these gifts are again active. We need to trust in God daily and, whether we are well or sick, we need to believe in prayer. Christ can still perform miracles of healing. It is a matter of drawing a dividing line between that and the over-zealousness of fanatics and sects.

The following considerations may help:

1. Every inexplicable miracle of healing is capable of a double interpretation; i.e. we cannot easily discover which of two spirits was at work. Christ healed by divine power and handed it on to His followers. But there are demonic powers which do not just exist in the imagination of frightened men. They also can work miracles. The world in which the early Christians lived was full of them. In the temple of Serapis at Alexandria many people were

healed in a remarkable manner and the pilgrimages to Epidaurus in Greece have become world-famous. A night's sleep in the sacred temple cured thousands. Appolonius of Tyana was a well-known itinerant preacher and miracle worker. People almost worshipped him as a god. There must have been at that time an overstrained psychic tension and activities similar to those which take place today in gatherings for healing.

From this it is clear that we need to inquire what power lies behind the miracle (cf Matt. 12: 22 ff. and Acts 8: 9 ff.). Is it fanatical fantasy, pagan religion or some secret demonic power? Or is it divine power and a real aid to health? Let us gladly admit that the one true God can have pity on people of simple faith, whether they belong to a fanatical sect or follow a heathen religion. "God maketh His sun to shine on the just and unjust."

2. The second point takes us on to a quite different plane. The Christian faith is in no way to be identified with a romantic glorification of the past. At the time of Christ medicine was a mixture of knowledge and an incredible amount of hocus-pocus. What the poor and suffering found in Jesus was indeed a blessing. His miracles of healing were a happy foretaste of the coming Kingdom of God. But the art of healing has made great advances in the course of the last few centuries and particularly in the last hundred years. Scientists have penetrated deep into the mysteries of nature with reverence and conscientiousness. For this Christians can be glad and recognise gratefully that here once more is evidence of the goodness and mercy of God in creation.

I shall never forget how Friedrich Dessauer, an expert on the subject, made this clear once in a course of lectures on Röntgen rays to Catholic and Protestant theologians. He said: "Do not despise science, you Christians. It has alleviated the suffering of millions and put an end to some diseases. This the Christians, favoured with their healing gifts, have not been able to do, for their work was as a drop in the bucket. It was often a sign of God's favour but not a thoroughgoing help. Would any of you undertake an appendicitis operation without an anaesthetic? Let us be thankful to God our Creator and Sustainer that He has given weak men the light of understanding so that they could discover wonderful remedies."

The Christian ought not to pour scorn on "school medicine". He does not know what courage and sacrifice many doctors have shown. He does not know of the open-minded research that faces every possibility with a view to discovering fresh help. Pious circles often show little gratitude for the progress made by genuine healers.

3. We need also to consider whether the Christian's distinction between the direct and indirect help of God is valid. God is said to help directly when the faithful pray, or at the laying on of hands, whereas the help is only indirect when a doctor prescribes a sulphonamide. But is that not to despise the lasting and ubiquitous creative work of God which we celebrate in the hymn "He knows a thousand ways to rescue us from death". Ought we not to thank God for the skilful amputation of a gangrenous leg as much as for a cure effected by prayer instead of medicine? Is the latter any more holy than the cure by a humble and helpful doctor?

In my opinion both should work together. We should pray and at the same time get the best medical help available. We should not try every doctor and only when that fails, resort to prayer as though it was just another medicine. I do not agree with the thesis that the invalid has to choose between these two methods.

Are we always sure that there is no simple and natural cure for an illness? Is our faith so strong that we think we can do without what God has given in the way of science and medical knowledge? It is quite a different matter when a patient, after calm, unhurried reflection comes conscientiously to the conclusion he must rely on prayer alone. This would, however, be the exception, not the rule for Christians. Saint Augustine taught that no miracle contradicted nature, but only what we knew of nature whereas Thomas Aquinas knew of God's help above and beyond the natural order.

It is wrong to say that things happen in the pentecostal movement whereas the church merely talks. Is the serious study and proclamation of God's Word nothing? Is it nothing that thousands of deaconesses visit and care for the sick and pray for them as well? Have we forgotten that Paul, who cherished all the spiritual gifts, placed love at the head of them? (1 Cor. 13).

4. There are, however, two errors committed by the spiritual healers and miracle-workers which are superstitious and must be resisted by Christians in the name of the Bible.

The first is that all illness is caused by sin and can be cured only by faith and prayer. This is nowhere to be found in the Bible. From Paul's letters we find that there were sick folk among the Christians. "Are we asserting," says Dr. Lechler, "that Paul, Timothy and Trophimus were heretics? If Timothy's stomach-ache had been due to lack of faith Paul would certainly have reminded him of it and not prescribed medicine" (cf. Phil. 2: 25-27; 1 Tim. 5: 23; 2 Tim. 4:20). Paul himself is the best example. Most commentators agree that the "thorn in the flesh" that "buffeted" him was a disease of the body (2 Cor. 12: 7). Sufferers could well learn from him to be content with God's mercy and to bear their ills to the glory of God. Of course there is a connection between sickness and sin, but it is not often direct and mostly cannot be seen in the individual. The connection is shown more in the general lot of man whose suffering is a foretaste of death (cf. John 9: 3). It is short-circuiting the truth to say that the devil is at the back of all disease. Sin separates us from God; sickness does not necessarily do so; on the contrary, many are refined by it and find a faith through it.

During the war I met a wounded soldier at the central dressing station. He had stepped on a mine which had blown his foot off. I was commiserating with him when he replied: "I have learnt something from it that I shall never forget. I had not been to church nor thought of God for ten years. Now God has called me and I will follow even though it will be only on one foot."

Those unhappy people who in their meetings try to force God to give them health are not aware that they are succumbing to a new idol, the *idol of health*. If we do get better it is because of God's free gift. Neither our faith nor anything else can force Him. "Faith does not perform miracles, it receives them."

The second error many of the movements for healing make is a dangerous one. It asserts that if the patient does not get better or falls ill again it is because he hasn't enough faith. What a convenient excuse for the unsuccessful quack and how cruel for the luckless patient! He has quite enough to bear and is often exhausted by his long sufferings, and now he is told pharisaically, "You are no child of God; you have no faith." What kind of pastoral care is it when a healthy man plunges a helpless sufferer further into the abyss of despair? We think of Christ's words, "Whosoever shall offend one of these little ones . . ." (Matt. 18: 6).

5. We see from this chapter that faith means seeking God and His Kingdom above all else. Superstition, on the other hand, directs people away from God. It encourages them to desire, seek and actually attempt to force things to happen (e.g. healing). Narrow is indeed the road of faith and we need constantly to pray: "Lord, I believe, help thou mine unbelief!"

If we maintain this attitude, we evangelical Christians need not at the same time be too serious and resigned. We can rejoice at the healing offered in the Bible to the faithful. We can confess that God hears prayers and works miracles in our church for which we can praise Him. Elias Schrenk was healed by a genuine miracle at Männedorf in Switzerland, and many others were healed by Father Stanger in Möttlingen and Pastor Blumhardt in Bad Boll. Miracles can happen through men of simple faith without any fuss being made. They are performed not by "star" healers, not in large assemblies, but by the quiet prayers of a small group (Jas. 5), or a whole congregation where the sick person is mentioned by name. The main thing is not the miracle, but the wonderful love of God who helps in a way we do not understand. The patience with which sufferers bear painful diseases and thereby inspire others is as wonderful as a cure. I remember two middle-aged women who were permanent cripples. They lay in bed year after year racked with pain. They preached a better sermon than many I have heard. Their room was a haven of peace. I went to it after listening to all the complaints, quarrels and protests of the other inmates. These two did not complain. They enquired about my work and the congregation whom they had very much on their heart. The man in charge of the old peoples' home in which they lived said he would have given up the job but for those two women. They glorified their heavenly Father through suffering.

Blaise Pascal's prayer makes a fitting conclusion to this chapter. "God, I pray not for health, not for sickness, not for life, not for death but that Thou wilt use my health, my sickness, my life, my death for Thine honour."

7

Lourdes, Fatima, Konnersreuth

IN this connection something should be said about the miracles of healing at Roman Catholic centres of pilgrimage.

The nun Bernadette Soubirous died at Nevers in central France in 1879. In 1933 at a solemn Mass in St. Peter's in Rome she was beatified. When I was in Nevers I gazed for a long time on her slight figure with its noble features full of suffering. Her body was exhumed twice and each time it was found not to have decomposed. On the coffin was an inscription to say her face and hands were covered in wax.

As is well-known, when she was fourteen years old she saw in a grotto of the Spelunkenberg, near Lourdes, the vision of a beautiful lady in a white dress with a blue girdle and a wreath of golden roses round her bare feet. She appeared no less than eighteen times and gave orders that a church must be built there and people must come in procession; also that she was to dig into the floor of the grotto with her bare hands. A thin trickle of water appeared and gradually swelled to a strongly flowing spring. Pressed by the priests and police, she told them, after much hesitation, that the lady had said her name was the "Immaculate Conception". That was in 1858, four years after the papal court had promulgated this dogma.

What has become the world's greatest place of pilgrimage started decisively with the sudden cure of a half-blind workman named Bouriette, and a child who had been ill for two years, both cures being effected by the water from the grotto. Even the Empress Eugénie sent for some of the water for her sick "Loulou". Enthusiasm spread like wildfire. In spite of the ban imposed by the prefect of police, as many as twenty thousand people at a time assembled at the grotto when Bernadette was praying there. Today there are about three hundred hotels and hostels, and pilgrims to Lourdes number between two and three millions a year.

At first there were a great number of cures. A commission of priests and doctors had to judge the cures as "inexplicable, immediate and lasting" before they could be accepted as genuine miracles. Cataract and consumption of the spine were among the diseases cured.

In spite of the increase in the number of pilgrims, the number of cures has declined. Up to 1914 there were a hundred a year; now there have not been more than two or three over several years. Of course hundreds feel better in themselves both spiritually and physically for a few weeks or months. I have never seen anyone healed in Lourdes, but I admired the discipline and joyous confidence of the processions accompanied by their priests and nurses. Prayers are held at six a.m. and eleven p.m. at the grotto and in the churches, and great reverence is shown. In the main church there is a huge figure of a hooded madonna painted above the small crucifix. It shows the transfigured face of Bernadette. Sincere Catholics are chief among those who complain of the tawdriness and worldly lust for gain that are displayed in such places. Not the least among them is Alexis Carrel, the Nobel prize winner who re-found his faith at Lourdes.

Medical science must be able to explain every process in terms of a natural cause. In the case of Lourdes, it points out the tremendous emotional excitement to which the pilgrims are submitted. Great tension exists in such places. There are stories told by happy people who have experienced a miracle and who have become voluntary nurses. Loud chantings rend the air; expectation is intense. The scientist is not surprised that miracles take place, i.e. that mind triumphs over matter. Of course there are some healings that are entirely inexplicable, but I am assured by doctors that there are patients in every clinic who get better for no evident reason, though not so quickly as in Lourdes.

Protestants will be specially cautious in their judgment. They are not so accustomed to appearances of the Virgin Mary such as the Catholic Church recognised in the "beautiful Lady". Even stranger is her description of herself as the Immaculate Conception which appears to be an attempt to get divine authority for a human doctrine. The present glorification of Mary seems to take away from the work of Christ who alone saves us. The intimate relationship between Bernadette and her Lady seems more like the eroticism of a young girl than the relationship recommended in the Bible (cf. the rejection of Jesus, John 20:17). "touch me not"

In spite of these objections, we must be aware that a loving God does not confine His gifts to those who have the right theology. Through the veil of too much worship of the Virgin and seeking after a miracle, there shine, even in Lourdes, instances of His favour to the poor despairing sick. Many a priest will certainly have consoled a disappointed patient with the words, "My grace is sufficient for thee". In her agony on her deathbed, Bernadette cried, "The spring is not for me!" In this world, the goodness of God and our sin, faith and superstition are intimately bound up together.

If we now turn our attention to Fatima, a place of pilgrimage in Portugal, we see similar remarkable appearances of the Virgin resulting in great excitement and a new stirring in the whole Catholic Church.

The events of Fatima are even more remarkable than those in Lourdes. On May 13th, 1917, three peasant children saw a beautiful young lady between fifteen and eighteen years old, dressed in dazzling white with golden braid on her cloak and a rosary. She was standing above a holm oak on the high desolate Estremadura plateau. Lucia was ten years old and had often seen apparitions, including angels. She stimulated the other two, Hyacinth aged seven and Franz Marto aged nine. They talked with the heavenly apparition for at least ten minutes. Many other visions followed and people began to flock to the spot. They saw in the clouds the "immaculate heart of the Virgin" surrounded by a crown of thorns. One day Mary promised a convincing miracle "so that all might believe". On October 13th in the same year, the miracle of the sun occurred following a snowstorm with lightning and a wonderful aroma. Between sixty and seventy thousand people watched the sun revolving more and more rapidly till it formed a wheel of fire giving off flames and rays of light.

Two of the children have now died. Lucia works in a Spanish convent as a nun. A huge church has been built in Fatima where confessions can be made in twelve languages. In the wide open space leading to it a hundred to two hundred thousand pilgrims are often gathered. On November 17th, 1942, Pope Pius XII fulfilled the Virgin's request. He dedicated the whole earth to the immaculate heart of Mary. Every Catholic Church in the world holds appropriate services and confessions in order to give satisfaction to the heart of Mary. After some opposition the government and the Church combined to give enthusiastic support to the new impulse stemming from Fatima. The same thing did not happen over Heroldsbach in Germany.

The small village of Konnersreuth in Oberpfalz (Bavaria) was the scene of a similar occurrence. Theresa Neumann (1898-1962) was an ordinary, fresh, healthy young girl until March 10th, 1918, when there came a great turning point in her life. She was helping to pass up buckets of water during a fire and had stood for a long time in the cold and wet. Suddenly she fell and felt a sharp pain in her back, apparently due to some damage to the spine. She grew worse, with alternate convulsions and vomitings until at the end of five years, she went blind. On April 29th, 1923, the day when Theresa of Lisieux was being beatified, she was suddenly cured of her blindness. On May 17th, 1925, she was suddenly cured of her spinal trouble. She believed that Saint Theresa had appeared and spoken to her. In 1926, the marks of Christ's wounds appeared on her body. The nail marks on the back of her hands were first in the form of a circle and then square. She ate and drank less and less. After 1927, she existed on a small daily portion of the host. Dr. Seidl and four nuns from Mallersdorf spent a fortnight in her house to examine her. The nuns took an oath of secrecy both before and after. During this time she bled freely every Friday. She lost several pounds in weight but later recovered to her former weight of about one hundred and twenty pounds. Her family refused to allow a further examination in an ordinary clinic, though the diocesan authorities in Regensburg urged it.

There were numerous other extraordinary occurrences. Theresa went through the whole experience of Good Friday and heard Jesus and the Apostles speaking in Aramaic. She gave many proofs of clairvoyance and telepathy, and healed a few people by taking their diseases on herself. These appeared in her body at the corresponding places. Father Fahsel, who is to be found among the pilgrims every Friday, recounts that when he was about to hand her the wafer, it disappeared out of his hand and he saw it hovering over the tongue of his communicant. Luise Rinser has written a widely-read book about Konnersreuth. She has a high regard for Theresa and says she was by no means hysterical. She was a natural, stubborn and fallible child like the others. You meet her as a sane person, loving truth and greatly favoured from above.

Formerly thousands were allowed to pass before her bed because she had shared in the sufferings of Christ, but in recent years this has been forbidden. I visited Konnersreuth on Good Friday, 1962, and noticed that the village had remained poor and unspoilt. Everyone, young and old, spoke of Theresa with respect. It was well known that her two brothers had been involved in illicit wine dealings after the war and had been convicted in court, but no one saddled Theresa with it. Out of freewill offerings she founded a college for men called to the priesthood late in life and it is now flourishing and giving many priests to the Church Her old pastor, Naber, enjoys universal esteem.

It is understandable that scientists like Professor Ewald of Erlangen should prefer to have natural explanations. It has been pointed out that Naber often put questions to her, such as "Isn't that what the voice said?" One of the enthusiastic members of the Konnersreuth Circle was the orientalist, Professor Wutz, who died in 1938. He often put questions to Theresa about the Aramaic words of Jesus. It cannot be entirely ruled out that tapping of the unconscious had something to do with it. The question arises too whether Theresa was really picturing the events of the years A.D. thirty and thirty-two, or only describing what she had heard in Church or Sunday School. As regards her refusal to take food or even drink, there are similar reports of the contravention of natural laws among both Indians and Europeans (Katherina Emmerich).

The objections Protestants raise lie deeper. Does God really want such a life and such a demonstration of the miraculous? Is there not, as Paul found, a "neglecting of the body, not in any honour to the satisfying of the flesh" (Col. 2: 23). Is it not a greater sacrifice to serve the sick simply and selflessly without stigmata or any special signs and wonders?

Or was Theresa destined to have an extraordinary charisma of bearing others' sufferings, of living above the natural world, as Theresa of Lisieux taught? Ought we practically-minded Protestants, with all our common sense, not to learn and rediscover what we have lost? Do we not find similar thoughts and dealings in serious Protestant circles? And is this not biblical?

We shall do well in our churches not to reject too hastily such questions, but rather to seek earnestly for an answer that is in accordance with our faith. The Catholic Church itself has not yet given a final answer, in spite of the approval of highly-placed churchmen like Cardinal Faulhaber. Every Catholic is still free to believe in either natural or divine causes. *Private revelations* are not included in the universally binding dogmas of the Church.

8

Belief in Demons, Witches and Angels

HITHERTO we have only spoken of the existence of the spirits of the dead, real or supposed. Without investigating the belief in demons, witches and angels, we cannot fully understand what Justinus Kerner called the "upsurge of the spirit world into ours".

Demons and Angels

The Age of Reason maintained the unambiguous point of view that all such notions were pure fantasy arising out of the fears of primitive man. There was no place for them in the laws of nature. Just as God Himself was now, according to David Friedrich Strauss, "in need of somewhere else to live", so were the angels and demons of the supernatural world.

Modern psychology and psychiatry are overwhelmingly of the same view. They talk of neuroses and psychoses and projection of the inner world into the outer. They explain the sudden and frequent outbreaks of epidemics in this field as due to "infection" and "accumulation", something similar to "induced madness". Peter Hofstätter's psychological dictionary does not contain the word possession, whilst parapsychologists refer to possession by evil spirits as "states of psychic pressure" (Theodor Constantin, Oesterreich), or evidences of split personality (Bender). Demons and their workings are as little subject to scientific proof as God Himself. Only a few modern doctors and psychotherapists like Dr. Alphons Maeder (Zürich) or Dr. Alfred Lechler (Oberursel im Taunus) take the view that we are here in the presence of an inexplicable survival, a reality that transcends the individual human soul.

The evidence we find in the Old and New Testaments is equally clear. Here the world is not conceived of as static, as subject to unalterable laws that admit of no exception. The whole course of the world is represented as dynamic and dramatic, a continual struggle between the powers of good and the powers of evil. Even though the faithful believe in the ultimate triumph of God, angels and devils are real to them.

But in this respect there is no firm line laid down in the Bible, one which is literally the same from the first page to the last. Whereas in the older parts of the Book of Job the devil is part of God's court and actually represents His interests, later on, other ideas appear which give a different conception. The devil, or Satan, becomes the enemy, the adversary, the calumniator and agitator. He seeks to drive a wedge between God and man. He is Lucifer, the bearer of light, who, at the beginning of the world rebels against God and sets up a rival kingdom. Unremittingly he persecutes the people of God and uses all his wiles to win over Christ, the Champion of light who, he senses, will conquer him in the end (Matt. 4: 1-11). Christ Himself sanctions this view when He talks of the kingdom and house of Satan which can only be taken when the head has been overcome (Mark 3: 23-27); likewise when He sends an answer to Herod, "Go ye and tell that fox. Behold, I cast out devils and I do cures today and to-morrow, and the third day I shall be perfected" (Luke, 13: 32). Indeed His whole mission can be summed up in the words of John, "For this purpose the Son of God was manifested, that He might destroy the works of the devil" (I John, 3: 8). He trans-mitted this power to His disciples and to the early Church. Even the keenest critics of the Bible agree that Christ's mastery over demons and His power to heal diseases rest on firm historical grounds.

How this fact is to be evaluated and explained is a matter of some controversy among theologians. Bultmann and Käsemann have rejected the idea of angels and devils along with the med-ieval picture of the world in three storeys. At the same time they do not reject the frightening power of purely subjective ideas of devils. G. Mensching says that belief in devils is a mythical interpretation of experiences that arise from the many dangers besetting human existence. G. Gloege asserts that demons are not spirits that can be met with in the world, that can be observed and described calmly, but rather a misuse and misunderstanding of life. When he says that life creates demons as God creates angels as expressions of all earthly happenings, he approaches more nearly to the pre-existentialist philosophers' conception of reality (cf. Psalm 104: 4).

In his bulky volumes of dogmatic theology, Karl Barth warns believers that they may fall into two errors, each of which takes bitter revenge later on. They may regard the question of demonology in the same light as the idea that the earth is flat, and so de-mythologise too quickly; or they may take the matter too seriously and give such a wide interpretation of demons that they admit them to the household of faith on the same level as God and the angels. If we ignore demons, they deceive us by concealing their power till we are ultimately forced once more to fear and respect them. If on the other hand we fear and respect them as being absolutely real, then by that very fact they have deceived us and concealed their true character as liars. Then we may try ignoring them again and so be again deceived! Lying, worthless though it is, exists as though it had life and substance and was a powerful, spontaneous and tendentious person. It founds and organises its realm. Demons are its exponents, they form and fashion lies in thousands of ways. In this the devil appears as God's ape, trying to copy and equal Him. It is our duty, therefore, to hold fast to the true God, to fear, trust and love Him alone and above all else.

From this we see that the views of psychiatrists and psychologists on devil possession are well founded and Christians may very well be thankful for every cure effected by scientific means. We must not forget either that discoveries about our physical body have revealed new connections. It is now well known that schizophrenics, who suffer from a split personality, are inclined to think in terms of devils and demons, and that this mental derangement can often be successfully alleviated or cured by electrical means or by the use of drugs.

The theologian, however, is bound to ask the doctor whether this way of regarding life takes in its whole breadth and depth. Is it not now generally accepted that the scientific method touches only one aspect of reality? May there not be, below the region of depth psychology, another depth which still baffles our methods of research? Is there not a danger that, for people who dismiss the devil in their daily lives, God will become the product of our mortal humanity and be discounted without substance?

In Faust, Goethe makes fun of the petty-minded bourgeois who only live on the surface of life: "They never feel the devil near until he has them by the throat".

About this, however, as about the question of the transmigration of souls and astrology, Goethe remained in an uncertain frame of mind which he often relieved with humour. The great Russian writer, Dostoievski, has thought more deeply about demons and with a greater sense of urgency. In his two novels, *The Demons* and *The Brothers Karamazov*, he gives a penetrating description of the human heart involved in demonic toils and

98

opens up fresh vistas into the depths of human personality.

It is no derogation of Christ to say that He shared the current scientific views of the world in which He lived, e.g. that the earth is flat. As Karl Heim reminds us, He took upon Himself for our sakes the limitations of our human existence. But the question of demon possession goes deeper. It depends on what view of man's nature we take and on the powers he is up against. Everyone must decide for himself. My belief is that Jesus was a keen-sighted realist who knew every trick and artifice of the feudal lords, business men and church authorities and everyone around Him. At the same time He lived in such close touch with His heavenly Father, that He not only understood God and the world in their true light, but the underworld of spirits as well. If He had regarded devil-possession as one of the diseases to be found in the casebook of a psychotherapist, would He not have been as ineffective as Don Quixote tilting at his windmills? The Teacher of the true faith would then have become a victim of superstition Himself.

Jesus certainly had revolutionary things to say about the old ideas of demonology. (Mark 7: 15 ff.), and we ought not to use the devil as an excuse (Gen. 3: 13); but behind all false talk of the devil there lies a hidden power. People suffering from possession by evil spirits show many of the usual signs of inner pressures being worked out, but these pressures are to be considered against the background of a demon-infested world. Let us look at some modern cases of people suffering from this form of torture.

A deaconess, a fine and devout woman, begged me to visit her seventy-year-old sister who was suffering from severe nervous trouble. She was sitting calmly in an armchair. At first the conversation passed off quite naturally. She seemed a friendly old soul and enquired in a kindly way after my family and church work. Then she had a sudden seizure. Her distorted features resembled those of an old man, dissolute and full of hate. The oaths and curses she hurled at me were indescribable and she got up from her chair in a threatening attitude. I could not imagine how she could have picked up words one only heard in the lowest quarter of the docks. Recovering from my first shock, I began to pray, hardly knowing what I said. Gradually her shrieking grew less and she collapsed in a heap of weeping misery. I visited her several times after that but no further attacks occurred while I was there. It was not a proper cure, for she died in an institution.

There are many such examples one could quote. The Biblical

story of the man possessed by a legion of devils (Mark 5) is particularly instructive, according to Kurt Koch who has made a thorough study of this subject. He thinks that this story, strange and even amusing though it may have seemed to people at the time, contains a series of typical traits which, unfortunately, are still met with today.

1. The victims defend themselves strongly against any contact with the name of Christ, the scriptures or prayer. This resistance is quite different from that of a person suffering from a psychosis due to false religious notions.

2. Unusual changes of features, way of talking and bodily attitudes during an attack. It often seems as though several spirits are at work at once, ("My name is legion, for we are many.")

3. Superhuman strength is noticeable. I once watched three strong warders having difficulty in holding down a small, emaciated man in a home for psychiatric treatment near Zürich.

4. Spirits driven out try to find another place. Animals in a stable become restless after someone has been healed in the house.

5. Superior intelligence and powers of second sight can be observed. In the New Testament the demons recognise Christ as the Son of God before the disciples do.

6. When an exorcist who is empowered by the Spirit masters an evil spirit in the name of Jesus, the cure is sudden and complete, unlike cases of mental disturbance (cf. Blumhardt, see p. 105).

7. Convinced and practising Christians are seldom devil-possessed, unless it be by relatively short attacks which are soon overcome.

As we have already seen, Koch laid great stress on what he called "occult affliction". By that he meant such occult activity as spell-binding or making a pact with the devil. It produces serious psychic upheavals. Depression, melancholia, frenzy, despair and a split personality result, as in other neuroses and psychoses. He is of the opinion that occult affliction also produces intermediate powers such as haunting and clairvoyance. He insists that this idea lies beyond the range of medicine and psychotherapy. It is a *theological* idea. For the theologian, magic is not only the outmoded activity of primitive man, but a definite decision to defy God, to dominate Him instead of praying to Him. It is not the pardonable superstition of ignorance but a union with the world of demons, a faith against a faith. Magic is not only the neutral, non-ethical use of the hidden powers of nature and human nature but also belongs, by its anti-God attitude, to the *civitas diaboli*, the realm of Satan.

What is worse, Koch has found in the course of his pastoral work that these occult afflictions are inheritable, like psychic disorders. The solemn words of the decalogue, "who visits the sins of the father on the children unto the third and fourth generation" (Exodus 20: 5), are literally true in this respect. One example will suffice.

During an evangelistic meeting a young woman got up and complained of psychic disturbances and weariness of life. Furthermore she was subject to fits which the doctor had said were not epileptic. He had diagnosed them as anxiety conflicts. Since medical treatment had brought no relief, she was seeking spiritual advice. Reminiscences of her family history brought strange occult connections to light. Her great-grandfather had been a spellbinder and had hanged himself. Her grandfather, who had continued the practice of spellbinding, had been crushed by an overturning hay wagon. His brother had been kicked to death by a horse. His son had been a cattle-charmer. He had cast a spell on three-quarters of the cowstalls in the village. After strangling his wife, he committed suicide. His sister had jumped into a well in front of the house and drowned herself. Now, this woman of the fourth generation was having these mysterious attacks.

A murder, two fatal accidents, three suicides, that was the terrible story of her family.

Koch points out that these people were not schizophrenics or sufferers from manic-depressive insanity, but sturdy peasants in the prime of life. He suspected devil-possession because this young woman became a Christian and, as far as his several months of observation went, remained free from attacks. In the village itself, however, the inhabitants raised an iron bulwark of resistance to anything to do with religion.

Belief in Witches and Witch Hunting

When we know about all these obscure things we can better explain the question of belief in witches and being bewitched.

It is unfortunately true that there have always been poor, misguided people who give themselves consciously to evil. They were driven to it by fear, misery, lust, avarice or a strong sexual urge. A formal pact with the devil signed in blood is not always essential to make the connection, though such cases do occur, even today. Koch tells of a member of his congregation who cut open his finger in a darkened room and wrote with his blood the words "Come, Lucifer". He was to receive 500 marks in return for his soul.

Dark and terrible as this is, the treatment of such people with fire, torture and the sword is even more terrible. In Soldan-Heppe's history of witch trials one reads with horror about the exquisite tortures to which often innocent people were submitted. The rack was used to tear out limbs; people were bound, raised in the air and dropped; grease was put on the soles of their feet and burnt off with fire.

In addition to all these horrors, there were fatal misconceptions. Pope John XXII declared magic to be a heresy. In medieval times this meant that everybody had to believe it. A heresy was thought of as more than just an individual crime. It was regarded as a general conspiracy against the foundations of Church and State. Fear of heresy was increased by the growth of the Cathar sect which rejected marriage and childbirth and favoured suicide. The unfortunate witches therefore were included in the cruelties of the Inquisition. In 1484, Innocent VIII issued his infamous bull against witches which gave rise to all kinds of fears of superstition. Henrich Institoris and Jakob Sprenger, in their book *Malleus Maleficarum*, laid down the most horrible methods for hunting out people and torturing them to death. It is thought that between 1575 and 1700 about a million people were killed for this reason, mostly women. A quarter of them were killed in Protestant areas, for both Luther and Calvin had urged the severest punishment for them, while lawyers and theologians drew up a special form of trial. The Jesuit Father, Friedrich von Spee (1591-1635) and the lawyer and philosopher, Christian Thomasius (1655-1728), were among the first to stem the flood of drownings and burnings. The last witch to be burnt in South Germany was Maria Schwägelin in 1775.

Apart from a man like Konrad von Marburg, the inquisitors were by no means narrow-minded fanatics. They were caught up in a nexus of complaints, calumniation, local quarrels and even self-accusations. The urge for self-destruction exists in man side by side with the urge for self-preservation.

There was another factor which we have recently got to know about. It is a disease-spreading drug which was widely used in the middle ages, chiefly by women. A liquid or ointment was made out of boiling henbane, hornapple, belladonna and other poisonous plants together. Twitchings, dreams of flying through the air and sexual excitement resulted from taking it. Many women could no longer distinguish between dreams and reality. Their confessions produced such wild notions as the witches' Sabbath on the Blocksberg and love affairs with the devil. Many of the accused were only mentally deranged, but this was entirely misunderstood in the Middle Ages. As late as 1850 such people were kept in prison, lying on straw and chained to the wall.

These distressing things have not been mentioned just to stir up cheap jibes against the faith and the Church, but because they still survive as unhealed traumata in the minds of nearly all European peoples. Many doctors, psychologists and pastors are still unaware how much harm is being done among ignorant and even among cultured people by the lingering belief in witches and witchcraft. It justifies C. G. Jung's belief that rationalism and superstition are complementary in this field also.

Those who have no experience of what goes on behind closed doors in towns and villages can find out from Kruse's book *Witches Among Us?* He treats the subject seriously though he only writes against witches from the rationalistic point of view. Black magic is practised by calling on the three names of the devil; useless quack remedies are prescribed for "sympathetic" cures; the eyes of photographs are pierced in order to produce blindness in the subject; love potions are brewed with urine and blood. I have confirmed that in nearly every chemist's shop in Germany you can buy the so-called "devil's drink", an evil-smelling liquid made with resin. It can only be used for unsavoury and magical practices and is utterly worthless.

Almost worse than the witches themselves, real or supposed, are the hunters of witches. They pretend to be working for the forces of good while provoking gossip and wicked tale-bearing which involve innocent and hard-working women. Red hair, deep-set eyes and knitted brows are all supposed to be the marks of a witch. The hunters earn a lot of money by their anti-witch campaign. They use old bird feathers, claws of wild animals, bones from the skeletons of people who have been hanged or beheaded, or hair from a suicide's head as a cure and often acquire a complete domination over their customers.

The report of a witch trial held in Ulzen in the Lüneburger Heide as recently as 1950, records how the children of a village in Lower Saxony shouted "Hi! Hi! Witch!" after a woman of forty-seven. The villagers said she had the look of a witch. She sued them in court. The defendants were a whole family consisting of the father, mother and a daughter. These *bewitched* defendants asserted that she had touched the cloak of one of them thereby causing heart attacks. Black crosses on the door-step, presumably drawn by the plaintiff, had brought trouble into the home. Cows had fallen sick and the hens had stopped laying. The father declared that his hair had stood on end and sweat had poured from his forehead.

During the trial, counsel for the defence and his colleagues received threatening letters from the opposition which said that defenders of witches would themselves become bewitched. In this year there were fifteen such trials in Lüneburg alone.

The temerity of the witch hunters is illustrated by the following example. A former miner was had up before the criminal court in Heide (Holstein). He had advised a farmer who thought his farm was bewitched, to have it exorcised. He came to the farm, ordered the farmer to cut off the head of a cock and drew circles round the farmer and himself with its blood, while muttering incantations. On another occasion he had prescribed a mixture made up of various herbs for a patient who was suffering from nerves and sleeplessness. As this did not cure her, he had visited her again and asserted that his patient was under the influence of an *evil woman*. After locking all the doors, he poured out a liquid into a bowl and lit it with the ninth match. A frightful stench filled the room and was supposed to have driven the evil woman away. Other patients, not only in Schleswig-Holstein but from as far away as Hamburg, were made to write with their blood on pieces of paper which they then had to throw into an open grave. In some cases his willing customers paid him as much as 250 marks. Such frauds are frequently met with still in South Germany.

Overcoming the Demonic

As an antidote to these practices, Kruse recommends intensive education. He thinks too that the State should intervene more and put a stop to lax court decisions favouring witch hunters, supporting magical practices and accepting false accusations.

All this is true enough and Kruse's work in this respect has been valuable. But it is far from adequate. What is needed in the first place is pastoral care. It is always the easily-led and morbidly self-concerned who have become entangled in their own desires and emotions, who fall victims. The removal of the causes of spiritual sickness and sin can only be accomplished by sympathetic understanding of the complexities, by calling in the aid of the psychotherapist where necessary, by private talks and inclusion in a group of people who have faith in God and the power of prayer. The best protection against fear of devil-possession and a false belief in witches is a lively, level-headed community that offers a place in its communal life. Only by prayer and fasting and the certainty that Christ is the Conqueror can people be finally cured of their fear of demons. Evil spirits cower at the name of Jesus or the offering of a prayer. Real freedom comes only through union with Christ.

The church needs again a call to repentance for having allowed the powers of evil to gain the upper hand. Apart from a few incurable fanatics who would still like to see witches burnt, the Catholic Church has already done much to make amends. Pius XII admitted in public audience that the Inquisition had been wrong, and his former private secretary, the Jesuit Father Robert Leiber, speaks with shame of this dark blot on the Church's history. He reminds us that the Church has now worked for centuries without using violence or torture.

The stricter circles of the Protestant churches must be particularly wary of going astray in this matter by drawing too theoretical and vivid a picture of the world of angels and devils. It is harmful to try and know too much about the angelic and demonic hierarchy. The treatise On Angels, by Dionysius the Areopagite, who lived about 500 A.D., and many of the writings of modern fanatical sects fall into this error. The reservations of the Augsburg Confession and Schleiermacher are to be recommended. We cannot observe these worlds from above or from outside them.

"How presumptuous it is of man to think he is the head of created beings!" says Adolf Schlatter. "There is an endless wealth of creatures beside and below us and then we come with our narrow, limited intellect. Is there to be nothing above us, just an empty space yawning between us and God?" Karl Barth is right when he points out that the simple process of what Osterhasen calls "demythologising" accomplishes nothing, in this respect, however proper it may be. We must understand the function of angels and devils. We only know of angels through their activity as beings sent to us, as the Bible says, as messengers and witnesses of God. We must never imagine they are independent spirits with an importance all their own. We must rely on God's kindness and care alone. Angels must never be allowed to obscure the healing work of Christ (cf. Heb. 1 and 2; E. Schick's Sacred Service page 10; W. Horkel, Message from Beyond, page 63 ff.).

One further consideration. As regards the belief in demons, we must repeat that it is unhealthy when Christians attribute every split personality and every mental disorder simply to the work of demons. It is highly dangerous when they too easily fall victims to occult powers and go in for exorcism of devils without careful checking. The confusion and spiritual distress caused by Hamann and his movement in Würtemberg should serve as sufficient warning. One of his followers committed suicide.

One further point is worth considering. It is doubtful whether fairy tales in which so many devils and witches, tortures and killings occur are really suitable for children. They may produce atavistic anxiety complexes, even in normal, healthy people who apparently take no harm from reading about stepmothers being drowned in a tub or witches being burnt alive.

Well-meaning and hard-working Sunday school and kindergarten teachers often implant these great fears in the tender heart of the child. Unfortunately they have not had sufficient training in these matters, so that their instruction sometimes resembles the medieval sermons on hell! Not that we should forget God's righteous anger against this world. It can and should be preached to grown-up and hardened sinners (Rom. 1), but not to defenceless little children, because the result is either an unintentional bewitchment, in the true sense of the word, or, in the course of time, the proud, intellectual rejection of all these ideas by the masses. Too much preoccupation with the notion of devils leads to superstition and unbelief, not to a true faith and trust.

However much one may regret the obviously unhealthy state of people apparently bewitched or devil-possessed, the diabolical effect of what Luther called the "white devil" (cf. Matt. 4: 5 f.), is considerably worse. The greatest triumph of evil is not seen in the occasionally horrifying methods of occultism but in the great false *ideologies* that hide behind promises of happiness to mankind. Dostoievski saw them become the rage in Russia and Europe. They capture the enthusiasm and faith of millions. But faith means recognising the world for what it is. These great Utopias, whether they call themselves nationalism or collectivism, atheism or materialism, all misunderstand reality. They leave men still unhappy. Professor Helmut Thielike pointed out long ago the warning contained in the suffix "ism". From a world point of view there is an idol, a false god, behind every "ism" which claims to be absolute and therefore upsets the divine order of things.

It is understandable that trained theologians and parsons view occult phenomena with reserve. Real pastors will care for the lost sheep and also accept Christ's readiness to help the masses. It was said of Him that He had pity on the people, i.e. those who were being led astray (Mark 6: 34; 8: 2).

Blumhardt's Triumphant Victory

Johann Christoph Blumhardt, a Swabian pastor in Möttlingen (Black Forest), has given a perfect example of the effect of wrestling in prayer for an almost lost soul. In his book, *Gottliebin Dittus* he describes how, as pastor of the village of Möttlingen, he was drawn into the affair against his will and on orders from a higher authority.

From childhood, Gottliebin had shown occult tendencies. A wicked cousin had wanted to initiate her into sorcery. When there was illness in the house, methods of sympathetic magic were used, although the parents were Christians and Gottliebin was receiving instruction in the Christian faith. The house itself seems also to have been placed under a spell. Powders, small packets of money and small bones which former occupiers had used for this purpose were found under the floorboards. For a time Gottliebin behaved well. She gave excellent service in several families, although she was already seeing apparitions. A disease of the kidneys provoked a whole series of other diseases, of the mind as well as of the body. She lay at home in Möttlingen in great suffering. The house was haunted by noisy spirits. She had seizures and fainting fits and began to see the spirits of the dead, among them a woman who confessed to her that she had murdered two children and buried them in the adjacent field.

Blumhardt never saw such an apparition, even Justinus Kerner only saw one. His visits to Gottliebin soon showed that some demonic power was at work. "While thinking thus, I was seized with a kind of frenzy. I jumped up, grasped her rigid hands, forced the fingers into an attitude of prayer and though she had fainted, I called her by name and yelled into her ear, "Put your hands together and pray: Lord Jesus help me! We have seen what the devil can do for long enough; now we want to see what Jesus can do'." She woke up and the seizure left her, but that was not the end. It was only the beginning of a struggle which lasted more than eighteen months.

Again and again her features were distorted into threatening looks, and strange voices came from her lips, some cursing, others pleading for mercy. Blumhardt admits he felt tempted to try magic, but he stuck to his purpose of employing only the weapons of prayer and quotations from the Bible. He spent whole nights at her bedside, never without witnesses, and watched twelve, fourteen, twenty-eight, four hundred and twenty-five and even thousands of devils come out of her mouth.

Her condition changed from better to worse and worse to better. Towards the end of the struggle, the number of terrifying apparitions increased. She made several attempts to commit suicide. The doctor who attended her was nonplussed when he saw whole buckets-full of water being vomited. She had clairvoyant visions of fires and earthquakes, and finally there came out of her body a large number of pins, nails and knitting needles which racked her with pain. Once when Blumhardt was sent for, he was nearly suffocated by the smell of blood which filled the room. A broad stream was flowing across the floor and blood was trickling out of her ears, eyes and nose, and even spurting from the top of her head.

At length, during the Christmas season of 1843, the drama moved to its happy ending. Her sister Catherine and her half-blind brother also came under demonic influence. The sister was so wild that they had difficulty in holding her down and curses poured from her mouth. One demon called himself "Satan's Angel" and resisted stubbornly for a long time before Blumhardt's prayer won the day. At two o'clock in the morning Catherine bent backwards over the chair while the supposed angel of Satan, in a voice that seemed hardly possible for a human throat to produce, yelled, "Jesus is conqueror! Jesus is conqueror!" After this it seemed that the power of the demon was broken. The brother and two sisters grew calmer and Gottliebin gradually recovered completely in body and mind.

It is remarkable that Blumhardt was able, after a time, to entrust his children to her care. She became an excellent teacher in kindergarten and industrial classes. Later on, she came to live with the Blumhardts and was almost a daughter to him. She was a great help in nursing his patients, especially those who were mentally or psychically disturbed.

In judging this victorious struggle, one cannot measure this unique man by ordinary standards. Not every pastor could do what he did, however well-meaning. It must be remembered that he had to give everything to it and fight with great devotion, often with long fasts. It does not belittle him to say that, in the light of more recent discoveries, in medical knowledge, he made mistakes and sometimes conjured devils by his own ideas of demons. Dr. Michaelis, a Lausanne nerve specialist, agrees on this and has shown that Blumhardt often succumbed to the animistic environment and its ways of thought. Furthermore it is more than a century since his fight for Gottliebin and in that time psychology has made great strides forward. It is worth considering whether a modern psychotherapist might not have been able to help this unhappy child, at least at the beginning of her illness. He could not free her from sin and guilt; that is a matter for faith. But could he not have helped her to live a normal life?

The Christians will see in this more than the successful healing of a patient. Blumhardt was overwhelmed with gratitude and described it as being a wonderful victory over the powers of evil by the help of God. It is shown also in his subsequent pastoral work in Bad Boll which was so greatly blessed, and in the stimulus to a sound biblical faith which he gave to the whole Church and which is still operative today.

9

Divining Rod, Pendulum and Earth Rays

THE divining rod is a mysterious instrument whose use can be traced back as far as there are any records of human activity. The Chinese Emperor Yu is said to have known of it and used it two thousand two hundred years before Christ. It was in use among the Babylonians, Etruscans and Celts, and the Egyptians had magic wands of a similar nature. Aaron's rod is referred to several times in the Bible. At a later date, Hosea denounces those who use rods for superstitious purposes. "My people ask counsel at their stocks, and their staff declareth unto them" (Hosea 4: 12).

The Roman authorities had a strong dislike for water diviners. Juturna, the water nymph, was represented with a hazel rod in her hand.

In the Middle Ages every mine had its diviner who helped in finding sources of water and seams of ore. It is surprising that the great medieval doctor and philosopher, Paracelsus, took no account of the divining rod, though it would have been in line with his pantheistic mysticism.

The art of divining by pendulum is also very old. In late Roman times two pendulum diviners were punished because they used their pendulum to discover who the next Emperor was going to be.

Both kinds of divining are widespread today. There is scarcely a town or village that does not have at least one person who practices the art. The rod takes several forms. It may be a forked branch cut from a hazel bush, a piece of looped wire or a wire spiral. The pendulum consists of a gold ring fastened to a hair from a woman's head or a lump of lead or plummet on the end of a piece of string. (Diagram 6).

The modern name given to these people gifted with hyper-sensitive powers is "Ray Aesthetes". They form a very large body whose members are keen and serious lovers of their art. It is rightly called an art because, as with music, some are more gifted

Diag. 6

Hazel stick   Wire springs   Pendulum

than others. With insensitive people the rod makes no movement at all.

Diviners say that experiments made indoors never produce any results. There are too many sources of disturbance such as metal and electrical appliances as well as sceptics. It is best to go out of doors and into open country, if possible where there are no natural signs of the presence of water, e.g. a particularly lush green in the grass or bushes. Usually the diviner takes the rod in both hands, palms upwards, and bends it into a curve of unstable equilibrium. If water is present, the rod gives a slight movement downwards (in France upwards). If the rod is vertically above the source of water, it gives a violent jerk. As the diviner moves forward the movements diminish within a definite limit. The distance between the sharpest and weakest movement of the rod gives the depth of the spring below the surface of the earth. The relative violence of movement indicates the amount of the water supply. Experienced diviners can tell the amount of yield to the nearest litre per second. The pendulum acts in the same way for water and nearly all raw materials like coal, oil, lead, uranium, silver and gold.

What does this gift consist of and how can the manifest successes of diviners be explained?

There are many answers to these questions, some complementary, others contradictory. American experts, and Englishmen like Sir William Barrett, a founder member of the Society for Psychical Research, incline to the view that telepathy and clairvoyance are the explanation. They came to this conclusion because of the lack of any physical evidence for some successful experiments carried out by diviners on non-metallic objects which had been concealed.

Other experts have pointed out the psychological aspect of the problem. In many cases, the diviner knows little or nothing about geology. Every substratum is the same as far as he is concerned. He supposes that sources of water can be found under every field and even every house. He does not realise that under a town lying in a river valley there is a sheet of water spread

over the entire countryside. One could therefore bore anywhere
with success, though the depth would vary with the geological
formation. But the diviner likes to prove his art by saying
you must bore at a particular spot. Twenty yards further away
would be no use. He feels the inner tension of expectancy and
this expresses itself in muscular contractions prompted by his
ideas. The idea that the rod will move may set up small, unconscious reflexes which lead to the slight movement of the rod
out of its unstable equilibrium.

In addition, he may unconsciously notice surface indications
such as the presence of vegetation etc. The climate and geology
of Germany give a seventy per cent success for all borings. It is
not difficult therefore, to register divining successes which are not
genuine.

Many amateurs are aware of these psychological causes and
treat objections seriously. At the same time they can point to
successes that come from unexpected places. They explain them
by referring to physically ascertainable stimuli operating on the
diviner which many people would not notice at all, but which
could be felt by a sensitive or allergic organism, even in the
smallest quantities.

This was particularly true of a famous South West African
diviner named Von Uslar. In the course of several years, he
found about eight hundred sources of water in this extensive
desert country, a success rate of about 70 per cent. On March
12th, 1913, the then Colonial Office issued a report of findings.
After mentioning his failures, they referred to the few exceptional cases when Von Uslar found water in places which the
experts would give up as hopeless. The report refers to a boring
at Hope Farm which stands at the top of the pass over the Aua
mountains. Experts would scarcely have made borings here, yet
a yield of 1,200 litres an hour was found by Von Uslar who
always denied having studied the area. He had trusted solely to
the movements of his rod.

Carl Graf von Klinckowstroem, who studied this subject for
many years with a critical mind, has recorded a similar case. In
the salt mine at Riedel, near Hönigsen, a farmer named Bibow,
who was an amateur diviner, had such a violent reaction at a
point where the rock formation changed, that his rod broke. It
was the first time he had ever been in such a mine. At a depth of
650 metres he had shown the precise spot at which the salt
changed to anhydrite. There were no visible indications to help
him; on the contrary there were plenty of misleading factors
such as places in the gallery where the mine dust had fallen

away leaving bright patches of rock salt which shone in spite of the half light. These would easily have deceived a diviner if it had only been a matter of movement prompted by ideas.

During the experiment, the electricity was cut off. In order to verify the find, the mine manager had first to scrape off the dust from the mine at the spot where the diviner had noticed the change.

About 1930, the Stuttgart state geologist, Dr. W. Kranz, carried out experiments with a Dr. K. Oswald, who was both geologist and diviner. In spite of his previous scepticism, he came to the conclusion that Dr. Oswald did possess some *sensitive affinity with the soil.*

Let us take an example from France. The abbé André Mermet was known as the king of the pendulum diviners. He lived at Jussy, near Geneva. He published a number of testimonials from Swiss communities, engineers and airport directors for whom he had discovered sources of water or flooding by means of his pendulum. One incident is particularly interesting. During the First World War the great chocolate firm of Suchard was very short of fuel and finally tried boring in Switzerland, though that country is poor in coal. The abbé roamed over the mountains and presently announced the find of a seam of anthracite in the Plex plateau opposite the Dents du Midi. It was 280 metres below the surface. Many of the geologists were scornful of a priest thinking he could find coal among primary rock, gneiss and granite. The company's engineer, however, decided to sink a shaft and found a seam under a fall of rock that gave excellent anthracite. The Mermet gallery was worked over a period of many years. The abbé does not hold with parapsychology or any psychological explanations. He speaks only of physical stimuli which reached him through the medium of his pendulum. However it only worked for coal, oil and water.

When we hear of such astonishing events, we are bound to want to know what these stimuli are and how their physical nature can be ascertained. Here we shall be putting our finger in the fire, for these stimuli have given rise to the most heated discussion, not only between physicists and non-physicists, that would be bad enough, but even professional physicists and geologists are to be found on both sides. The following are the main points of dispute.

It is well known that the earth is a great magnet. The geographical north and south poles are not the same as the magnetic poles. There are magnetic fields covering the surfaces of the whole globe in an unbroken series which may, however, be diverted or upset by different rock formations, faults or chasms as well as by deposits of oil and ores. Magnetic storms can also bring about changes in magnetic fields which can be measured by a Smith field balance or other apparatus. Measurement is not easy. Accuracy can be destroyed by the passing of an electric train a long way off. Furthermore, the earth with its surrounding atmosphere is like a gigantic condenser. Its surface is charged with negative current while the air is charged with positive.

The potential and the drop in potential can also be measured. They are constantly changing, of course, with daily variations and with the seasons. Rain, thunder, smoke, or dust bring about these changes. So can radio emanations from the cracks in the earth's surface and damp cellars. Those who believe in divining assert that all these things affect the diviner more than they do the finest instrument, because he is a living, sensitive organism. Experts talk of "lines of stimulus" arising from disturbed areas (Kritzinger) or "earth rays" (Freiherr von Pohl), which are thought even to cause diseases ranging from depression, rheumatism and tuberculosis to inflammation of the meninx. The famous master diviners, Dannert and Freiherr von Rolshausen of Bonn attribute the growth of cancer to these lines and rays. The rod has even revealed cancer-infected houses whose inhabitants one after another died from this painful disease.

Dr. Jenny (Zürich) with other diviners showed that animals instinctively avoid these lines of stimulus. All the hens in one henroost slept on poles near such a line, but none slept on the pole above it. Divining experts are not agreed on the nature of these rays.

Most geo-physicists are very sceptical about these researches and assertions. In 1955 several scientists from the Medical Law Institute in Bonn collaborated in a series of articles published by Otto Prokop, in which they flatly rejected these ideas. Either, they said, these rays are well-known apart from any connection with the divining rod, or they are not subject to physical proof and therefore cannot exercise any physical effect.

These scientists have naturally based their findings on experiments conducted with diviners and have tested the favourable experiments others have made. The results were, almost without exception, negative.

One of the most important investigations was undertaken by Gassmann after the Second World War. He sent a number of water diviners through a field under which the Zürich water main lay. The report says that they were told it was there, but no one was allowed to know that anyone else was being tested. The pipe carried 1600 litres a minute. It was twelve millimetres thick and had a diameter of fifty-five centimetres. The top was 1.4 metres below the surface. None of them found it. On the other hand several found a pipe that was not there! They were obviously influenced by the manholes they could see.

On another occasion a diviner was placed in a locked cabin suspended from the roof of an enormous hangar in a factory. The cabin was moved backwards and forwards over a line of stimulus while he was to indicate the movements of his rod by a system of lights. At the end of the experiment, only criss-cross markings had been traced on the floor of the hangar. The diviner himself was obviously impressed by this negative result.

Equally remarkable was the lack of reaction a famous diviner showed when one of the testers approached him with a lump of uranite hidden in his briefcase, though uranite is strongly radio-active.

In all these experiments, the cause of failure might have been due to a variety of things. The diviners might not have been very skilful or might not have been feeling very well at the time, or they may have been unable to express their reactions in clear terms. At the same time, none of these earth rays have yet been discovered, nor has the human organism been shown to act as a catalyst that could record imperceptibly small impulses. The well-known professor of geology at Tübingen, Dr. Wagner, is convinced that there are certain people on whom variations in the subterranean structure do exercise an influence, especially in places where there is water or metal ores; but the explanation of the stimulus remains a matter for dispute.

It is natural with a subject of this nature that there should develop a variety of accretions of a superstitious and harmful nature round a nucleus of fact, or at least of observations worthy of examination. What are we to think when we hear of pendulum diviners who assert that divining can take place from one's arm-chair or that there is no need to be out of doors? They say it is enough to have a map in front of you which shows, by giving out these mysterious rays, where ore, coal or water is to be found! The abbé Mermet boasted that he had found springs and lost gold coins at a distance of 10,000 kilometres. By poring over his map he had found the spot where a girl lay drowned in a lake. Her parents and the police had been searching for a long time in vain. He was only one metre out, though the lake was a considerable distance away. It was not any kind of clair-voyance. A "head ray", i.e. a ray from the map and a ray from the girl had reached his head at the same time and shown him the right direction.

One expert pendulum diviner, Frank Glahn, called the pendulum the "brother of the rod". He produced some similar astonishing ideas. He and thousands of his followers believe that there are not only physical rays such as we have described, but that the human body is made up of such rays. These "od" rays were discovered by Freiherr von Reichenbach. They are said to surround the body like an aura and can be seen in the halo. They can also emanate from a photo or painted portrait. Information about life, death, health, sickness, character and destiny can be read from the features. The picture changes with the differing fate of the subject. Glahn went so far as to maintain that the photograph lives on with the person photographed, however far removed they may be from each other. An intangible ray reaches from the one to the other. From the picture of a child, its future mental and bodily state can be deduced. Even blocks made from a photo have this relationship to the person. The pendulum reveals the present, past and in many cases the future condition. "How wonderful!" he exclaims. "Test the miracle!" No one will be surprised to learn that in this man's writings there is a mass of cabbalistic, astrological and magical ideas all jumbled together.

All this would be harmless if pendulum divining were not so widespread and diviners did not meddle so often in medical affairs. From my knowledge and from facts given by Koch it is safe to say that, after the war, tens of thousands of women took a photo of a husband or son to pendulum diviners to know if their loved one was still alive. I know also of men and women pendulum diviners who even today have a clientele in far distant towns which includes rich and influential businessmen. One friend of mine went to a pendulum diviner. Without being asked, he gave him straight away a general medical report. "You have a weak heart and often feel pain there. You have stomach ulcers especially in the region of the duodenum; in addition you suffer from kidney trouble and your bladder is affected." This "patient" had not gone for this purpose and enjoys both excellent health and a critical mind!

It is easily realised what effect such a diagnosis might have on an unstable and sensitive nature. He will, in the first place, take as a diagnosis what is far from being proved. There are at least a dozen forms of heart disease and many complications which only a specialist knows about. In the second place, this unfortunate victim will fall into a state of anxiety every time something seems to go wrong in his body. He will think he has now got the disease and is seriously ill. Many of these lay-doctors would be horrified if they realised the consequences of their facile treatment. But their poor memory and lack of education protect them from any subsequent prickings of conscience.

The various forms of physical apparatus employed by diviners to assist their secret powers are highly dangerous. Dannert, a diviner from Hagen (Westphalia), who died recently, invented a combination rod which was supposed to respond infallibly to every form of disease. It was shaped like an enormous pair of tongs into which small glass tubes could be fitted. Into each tube he put one of forty different "elements" in such a small quantity that it was like a drop of water in a railway carriage. Each element corresponded to a disease. When the rays of the right element met the right disease the tongs would give a jerk and in this way diagnose the trouble. He elaborated his ideas by dividing the elements into three groups. Group one showed bone diseases and cancer; group two covered nervous troubles; group three dealt with all organic diseases.

This shows clearly how his ideas are rooted in magic and superstition. Without having any medical knowledge, he constructed a machine that was said to *know* all about every case. It did violence both to the sufferer and to the truth. The only difference between him and the medicine man with his magic wand is, that the former has a more mysterious technique and fails to acknowledge the findings of medical science. Whilst we are able to enjoy these every day, the medicine men of New Guinea know nothing of them.

When one thinks of the many "radiation implements" and forms of "protective apparatus" made in the factories, one can only marvel at the stupidity of men. I have before me the prospectus of an "electrified chain" which is said to cure malignant diseases. You have only to hang it round your neck and a disease you have had for years will disappear! Dozens of testimonials are printed in the prospectus. "No doctor could help me. My malignant stomach ulcers have now disappeared. I can now eat anything!" Another writes, "For months I suffered from vomiting and diarrhoea. I was cured in a few days." On the same page came this: "Constipation vanished like lightning."

Many of these trusting people may have experienced some relief but were they really cured?

Mention should be made of some of the forms of apparatus for warding off earth rays. One is called the Schweizer-Weber plate. It consists of two strips of metal foil which keep away all harmful rays when fastened under the bed. If people cannot afford this apparatus, the same result can be obtained by lying on a bed of bracken, but the bracken must be renewed every two months.

In order to protect the whole house, one should use the "North-South Rectifier" as supplied by a Bavarian firm. This small machine does not have to be plugged in as it has its own permanent magnetic field capable of being tested and measured by technical means. For this reason it remains active permanently and is cheap at eighty marks. In the prospectus the firm state that diviners and earth ray experts are in fundamental agreement that its high range of efficiency is due to the biological weakness of the earth rays.

Dr. Mannlicher, medical adviser to the town of Salzburg, is an expert on rays. He recommends an instrument you can make yourself. Place two small mirrors facing each other five centimetres apart. The rising earth rays are so irritated at being reflected from both sides that they are thereby rendered harmless! In one village I found a bar of copper one metre long buried in a stable. It had cost five hundred marks.

The most successful and widely used apparatus is the one constructed by Dannert whom we have already mentioned. It is called the "phylax". I opened one of these in the presence of a friend who had a diploma in physics. He broke into fits of laughter. The only contents were two wire spirals marked "out" and "in". As the spirals were short-circuited, these marks were meaningless. The instrument was sold at eighty to a hundred marks. Taking the value of the wire at half a mark and the elegant box at three marks, one can see what enormous profits these diviners are making. The effective protection offered by the apparatus was only ten to twenty metres in extent. This did not prevent Dannert selling one to the people next door, irrespective of the laws of interference of rays.

I witnessed an amusing occurrence at a meeting I attended. During a lecture to two hundred simple old folk, the diviner discovered a stream of water beneath the floor and walked over it among the chairs and tables. For the next lecture, the chairs and tables were arranged differently, but the confident diviner found water wherever he could conveniently walk between them with his rod!

The wife of a man I knew was only able to sleep at night when the phylax was fixed under the bed, otherwise she suffered from palpitations and nervous disorders. Without saying anything to her, my friend substituted a wooden box of the same size and shape. It proved just as effective. She only needed to

118

glance at the wonderful "guardian" under the bed to be sure of a good night's sleep.

I know of two people who died of cancer after much suffering because they trusted to this apparatus instead of going to a doctor. They paid dearly for their folly. A woman specialist told me that out of a hundred causes of cancer she had never come across these harmful rays as one.

There is one further case I will quote which had medical backing. It came before the court in Saigen (Mindelheim) in 1956. In his report on the diviner Jakob Müller, Dr. Beck, the senior medical officer of a child's clinic in Bayreuth, proved the existence of harmful earth rays. The electric cardiogram of a seven-year-old girl showed irregular heart beats clearly when the protective apparatus was switched off. When it was switched on again the irregularities ceased and her general condition improved at once.

Perhaps science has not yet pronounced the last word on these mysterious rays, but I think sensible people who dislike superstition would do well to observe the following rules in order to avoid incurring mental or bodily harm:

1. During experiments in water divining, whether in private or public, a trained geologist should be called in in every case. If the interested person insists on having a diviner, make sure the diviner has no financial interest in it and does not make use of magical practices.

2. Be on your guard against diviners who say they can recognise or heal diseases or foretell the future. We are dealing here with the dividing line between magic and the medium's talent. Error could lead to psychic disturbances or spirit possession. Koch rejects out of hand all diagnoses given through pendulum divining, whether it is a doctor, a parson, an engineer or a charlatan holding the pendulum. He bases his rejection on the cases of mental derangement he meets with in his pastoral work.

3. Give all vendors of protective apparatus a wide berth. People's fears, specially of cancer, are being nourished and played upon too much. The judgment of science is too uncertain as yet. Trust a local doctor who is well-known and takes responsibility for his diagnosis; or go to a psychotherapist or pastor who can give experienced help.

10

The Message of the Stars

NEARLY all civilisations have produced an astrology of one kind or another. For thousands of years there has been a constant stream of people who have believed in the stars, a stream that sometimes flowed broadly in open daylight, sometimes secretly through gorges and underground passages. We must therefore give a short account of astrology's long and varied history.

History of Astrology

1. Origins

Religion has been the begetter of all the arts and sciences. This is true both for astronomy, which studies the stars from a scientific point of view, and for astrology, which seeks to find a meaning in them for man. Both go back to an older form of *astral religion*. This is not the oldest form of religion, which is probably the belief in Mana, or force, as we saw in chapter one. A piece of bone, a stone or a piece of wood were all supposed by primitive man to possess some power. He divided objects into those that should be worshipped, those that were taboo and those that could be worn as amulets.

Between twelve and fifteen thousand years ago man began to observe the heavens. He invented explanations for the courses of the sun, the moon and the stars. It was not the mystery of the sun that first attracted him. Unlike us who live more in daylight, cave man was more concerned with the mystery of the dark and so with the fate of the changing phases of the moon. Full moon was obviously celebrating a triumph of its power. The waning moon was believed to be losing its power. Some wicked monster like a ferine wolf must be harrying and pursuing it. During the day it rests in the grave and on the third evening it rises again and appears as a thin sickle in the sky.

In calling it a sickle, we must remember that this implement was unknown to early man who used a different symbol. The crescent reminded him of a bull's horns. Evidence of this is seen in the large number of bulls painted on the walls of rock caves in France and Spain and on rock surfaces in the Sahara. Other animals are not depicted so often or so large. Thus the worship of the bull and of the moon became closely associated for many centuries. A Sumerian inscription of 2000 B.C. from Ur reads: "Moon who art the mighty bull". In Babylonia the bull was given wings to symbolise the moon's flight through the sky.

cow that jumped over moon!

In northern latitudes the new moon appears to our practised eye vertical. But the further south we go, the more horizontal it appears till it ultimately looks like a ship sailing over the waters of which the heavens were supposed to consist. This is the reason for the ships of the dead painted on the walls of the tombs of Egyptian and Mesopotamian kings. Then the ship sailing through the waters becomes identified with the fish. The tribes of New Guinea still worship a moon-fish god, and pisces, the sign of the zodiac, is represented by two horns or the two ends of a ship.

2. The Babylonians

That was how things were in the most primitive times. It was the Babylonians who first gave form and shape to the religion of the stars. They made the first attempts to develop in more detail the connections between events in the heavens and events on earth. The priest was first and foremost both astrologer and astronomer. The Tower of Babel is well known. It was not really a tower but a pyramid with seven terraces. Only the king and the high priest were allowed on the top where there was an observatory and a "dream chamber" with a statue of the god Marduk inside. It was here, as we have seen, that a pure young virgin spent New Year's Day dreaming about the future of the nation. Her dream was then explained and interpreted by the chief astrologer.

But considerable discoveries in astronomy were also made. By the year 2000 B.C. it was known that the morning star was the same as the evening star. Scholars had grasped the importance of the ecliptic, the great highway along which the planets moved. (Diagram 7).

Even among the Babylonians there were signs of serious error. While at first the courses of the stars were connected with the fate of kings and nations, as witness the star Regulus, and a high level was maintained, astrology got more and more entangled in a confused mass of individual statements, some of which were contradictory.

By 700 B.C. soothsaying books were in widespread use. They

Diag. 7
A kind of World Eye
1. *Original waters.*
2. *Firmament with sun, moon and fixed stars.*
3. *Water under the firmament.*
4. *World island and world mountain with Babylon in the centre.*
5. *Oceans.*
6. *Hell fire.*

were called *Omen Texts* and were based on the principle that if A happened, B was bound to follow. For example, if Jupiter is in conjunction with Venus prayers will be offered to the nation's gods and they will be heard and answered by Marduk and Sarpanit; or, if on the fourteenth of the month Sivan the moon is veiled and the east wind is blowing, war will break out and many will die.

From this time on, astrology became a *market astrology.* Answers could be brought to every question without reference either to experience or observed fact. Unfortunately this corrupt astrology with its superstitions was brought into Egypt and other countries. One must be cautious therefore in talking about the "wisdom of the ancient east", and check carefully everything that has been handed down to us.

3. The Greeks and Romans

The Greeks were the first to adopt a genuinely scientific and philosophical attitude towards the stars. The Pythagoreans, named after Pythagoras who lived in the sixth century B.C., discovered that the earth was round though, like their master, they thought the planets travelled on crystal balls. Democritus (c. 460-360) explained the milky way as congeries of stars. Eratosthenes (third century B.C.), calculated the earth's circumference to be 42,000 kilometres by using a set square and a stick. Aristarchus of Samos worked out a stellar system centred on the sun seventeen centuries before Copernicus. All these are major achievements of the human mind and they laid the foundations of genuine knowledge.

Later on these great discoveries of the Greek philosophers were forgotten. Somewhere between A.D. 85 and 160 Ptolemy wrote his

Almagest, so-called from its Arabic title. It was the standard book on astronomy for 1,500 years, while his *Tetrabiblos* was the astrologers' *vade mecum*.

The Romans were better at ruling than at philosophy or science. Their religion is impregnated with superstition and their studies of nature are far from exact, as witness Pliny the younger who was killed in the great eruption of Vesuvius in A.D. 79. He maintained that the stars are undoubtedly fed by mist from the earth because at half moon, spots can be seen on it and these spots are caused by the dirt sucked up from the ground by the mist. Roman agriculture was also conducted according to the confused regulations of the astrologers. There were very few critics who, like Cato the Elder, cried: "Away with your Mars and Venus, your Saturn and Jupiter! Fields must be dunged—that's the important thing." Cicero too, with his clear and logical mind, wrote against astrology in his book on soothsaying. "How many fortunes I remember being told about Pompey and Crassus, and even Caesar, which all asserted that they would die in old age, in their beds, and at the peak of their fame. I am surprised that there are still people who believe in such prophecies since those have been contradicted by what followed."

In his sixth satire, Juvenal (*c.* A.D. 100), makes fun of the all too assiduous women of the Roman aristocracy. "They trust completely the Chaldeans. What the astrologers say is believed as if it was an oracle of Jupiter Ammon. Beware of any woman you meet who carries a well-thumbed copy of a yellow astrological handbook. She won't ask any questions of others but she will give answers. If the calculations of Thrasyllos are against it, she will not budge, whether her husband is going to war or returning to his home country. If she thinks she would like to go for a walk to the next milestone she consults the book about the time. If the rubbed corner of her eye twitches she has her horoscope read and only then asks for some eye salve. If she is ill in bed, no hour for food is better than that recommended by the great Egyptian astrologer Petosiris."

But the triumphant march of astrology was not to be halted. Caesar Augustus had a coin minted with his sign of the zodiac on it—a ram. Tiberius and Caligula ordered senators with a bad horoscope to be put to death. Nero too was a passionate believer in astrology, which continued to flourish in the Christian era in spite of Constantine the Second's ban (350). It combined with the Venus-Isis-Sothis cult of Egypt and cults of other oriental countries. A Sicilian named Firmicus Maternus, who later became a Christian, published a book in A.D. 336 in which he laid down the aspects which would decide the fate of children born under them: i.e. whether they would become murderers, gladiators, lawyers, slaves, incestuous persons, etc.

As Roman society degenerated so astrologers became more brazen and coarse in their reading of the stars. Even the enlightened St. Augustine had much difficulty in freeing himself from their thraldom.

4. The Middle Ages and Modern Times

As we have seen, astrology came into Europe via the Arabs who had translated the works of Ptolemy. The Emperor Frederick II and his famous court physician, Michael Scotus, offer an example. In his Divine Comedy, Dante consigned the doctor to hell!

The Renaissance brought in a new vogue for astrology through its enthusiasm for classical antiquity. Bishops and even Popes were affected by it although many synods had condemned it. Paul III (1534-49), refused an alliance with France because the aspect of the stars at his birth and the French king's was against it. Every Italian prince and city state employed an astrologer. Even the Condottieri consulted one before setting out on their and agitated by his prophesyings."

In his introduction to Goethe's *Faust*, Ernst Beutler writes: "Renaissance man feels himself threatened by the stars. It is true in one sense that the Renaissance set him free, but fear of the stars replaced fear of hell and most people still feared both. The astrologer was the only one who could help and therefore he enjoyed a high place in man's esteem. A horoscope was as powerful as a newspaper is today. Whole nations could be stirred and agitated by his prophesyings."

The birth of Louis XIV, who later became *Le Roi Soleil*, was artificially delayed by doctors and nurses for nearly an hour till Morin, the court physician and astrologer signalled with a cloth from his observatory that they were to hurry on with the delivery. Subsequent events would appear to have justified his timing, for Louis became a great king.

The Reformation had to come to grips with astrology. Luther called it a "shabby art and subtle foolery". "Astrology," he said, "is no science. It has no principles and no proofs." On the other hand Melanchthon lectured on it and believed in it all his life.

In its heyday astrology affected architecture and art as well as literature. We have only to think of the Otto Heinrich wing of Heidelberg castle begun in 1556 with its figures representing the seven planets, or the famous frescoes in the Schifanoja palace at Ferrara. Dürer's "Melancholia" and da Vinci's "Last Supper" were both influenced by it. Even false prophecies could not shake people's belief in it. A Tübingen astrologer, Professor Stöffler, foretold a great flood on February 25th, 1524. There was great agitation everywhere in Germany. The Elector of Brandenberg and his whole court took refuge on a hill near Berlin and several Bishops had arks built. There was no flood, but the Peasants' War broke out the next year. False prophet though he had proved himself, he retained the esteem of the city.

Petrarch (1304-74) and the philosopher Pico della Mirandola (1463-95) were strong opponents, while Sebastian Brant (1475-1521) and Rabelais (1494-1553) vented their satire on it. At the beginning of his novel *Gargantua and Pantagruel*, Rabelais gives a "true and veritably undeceptive book" of prognostications by Pantagruel in which he pokes fun at the calendar makers. "On this year's diseases: This year the blind will see little; the deaf will become hard of hearing; the dumb will speak little; the rich will be better off than the poor; the healthy than the sick. Many sheep, oxen, pigs, hens, geese and ducks will die; less apes and camels will die but not such a violent death. Old age will be incurable this year because of last year; those with lung trouble will feel pains in their sides and those who have the falling sickness will often sit on chairs."

Erasmus of Rotterdam, the great humanist, (*c.* 1465-1536) had no good word to say for astrology. Astronomers like Tycho Brahe (1546-1601). Galileo (1564-1642) and Kepler (1571-1630) occupy a special place in Copernicus' new scientific outlook on the world, which had had a revolutionary effect. They devoted themselves to the new researches with great enthusiasm and were astonished at the vastness of the universe. Kepler, however, hesitated all his life between the old and the new thinking. He wrote in his *Tertius Interveniens*: "Astrology is a foolish daughter, but, great God, where would her mother astronomy be if she had not had this foolish daughter? and the world is even more foolish." He thought the astrologers' prophecies in the calendars were worth as much if not more than the conjectures of the politicians, but "One should realise that when God is angry it is no use the star-gazers talking of luck. They can help no one and do not know what will happen to the world but are like the stubble which the fire consumes."

On the other hand Kepler was repeatedly compelled to read the horoscope of his two masters, the Emperor Rudolf II and Wallenstein, and to publish his own calendars, for during the Thirty Years' War he received no salary. The Emperor owed him twelve thousand guilders. Privately, however, he still believed in reading the stars and his great work *The Harmony of the World* contains not only the brilliant calculations of the tracks of the planets but also highly abstruse things like the inhabitants on the moon, what sort of houses they lived in and what use they made of the walls of the huge craters, e.g. whether vegetables grew under their protection.

With the coming of the Age of Reason astrology declined in popularity. Chairs of astrology at the universities disappeared. The last lecture was delivered at Erlangen in 1816.

In the face of the triumphant onward march of exact science, astrology faded from people's minds. It became a subject of purely academic and historical interest. In his well-known book *Belief in the Stars and their Meaning* (1918) Boll describes it as both a science and a faith that belong to the past, though a not too distant one, which few people now know much about. He was only apparently right. He could not have suspected how wrong he was to be. The pendulum soon swung the other way. The shattering events of two world wars; the misery that followed, and the lack of spiritual roots in the mass of the people produced a fresh search for some solid foundation for life. Astrology came into fashion again. Wide circles rely on it and believe that it can foretell the future. Discussions about belief in the stars are widespread.

True and Alleged Relationships Between Man and the Stars

In these discussions one must be on one's guard against two possible mistakes. We must not take the findings of primitive astrology for granted, but at the same time we must not approach them from the rational or materialistic side only. The astronomer Henseling has good grounds for saying that on no other subject has so much thought and conflicting opinion, so much wealth and human endeavour been expended during the thousands of years it has held sway in every part of the world. Only the most superficial observer could characterise it as merely a matter of the fearful and unintelligent masses in search of certainty about the future. Throughout its history many of the finest and ablest scholars have been among its convinced adherents. Is it likely therefore that it could lack all content of truth?

Clearly the answer to this question must be in the negative. Some imperishable ideas lie at the root of astrology which are acknowledged or at least respected by serious scientists.

The first of these ideas is contained in the Greek word *cosmos* which implies that the world is not a meaningless, chance creation but an interrelated whole, a system in which every part fits into the rest and no phenomenon is isolated from any others. Everything, great or small, obeys the same laws. Spectral analysis shows that the same elements exist in the most distant stars as in our planet. These inter-connections apply equally to animate nature as to inanimate. One meaning and one inner harmony prevails throughout the cosmos, thought out and directed by a higher Spirit. It is far from being soulless. Goethe has given fine expressions to this in one of his poems:

> *When as throughout infinity*
> *The same repeats eternally,*
> *And all the joints of heaven's vault*
> *Are fitted perfectly together,*
> *Then joy of life from all things flows,*
> *From smallest stars as from the sun,*
> *While still amid the stress and strain*
> *Repose is found and rest in God.*

The Psalmist sings in the same strain: "O Lord how manifold are Thy works! In wisdom hast Thou made them all. The earth is full of Thy riches" (Ps. 104: 24).

Connected with this idea is a second one which views the world as *spiritual*. Whilst the universe is so vast that we are but tiny specks in it, *man* is still of supreme worth, even now that we are discovering that our solar system is only a small, insignificant spot in the Milky Way which itself is a hundred thousand light years long and fifteen thousand light years wide. It contains ten milliard suns and is only one of many such groups. Its neighbour is the Andromeda nebulae, 2,000,000 light-years away. They can barely be seen by the naked eye. Astronomers know of a hundred million such groups so far. How small then is man with his space travel! He is like a child who, wanting to explore Europe, wanders round the garden looking at molehills. And yet man is important; indeed he is a copy of the world order, the microcosm of the macrocosm. One heart, one mind, one living person, one human community is more than all the lifeless wastes of the star-set universe.

On an emerald green tablet to the Egyptian god Hermes Trismegistos (thrice great Hermes), these words are inscribed. "It is true and not a lie that the lower is as the higher and the higher as the lower for the completion of the one miraculous work."

The same idea is found in Psalm 8 though not within the

framework of a pantheistic infinity but of faith in a personal/ God who condescends to love the lowliest. "When I consider Thy heavens, the work of Thy fingers, the moon and the stars which Thou hast ordained, what is man that Thou art mindful of him? and the son of man that Thou visitest him?" The answer is not "a speck of dust" or "a cipher".

These two great ideas about the universe and man are confirmed by a train of observations which have partly revealed the laws of the cosmos to us and partly allow of intelligent speculation. A few examples will make this clear.

The Moon

We are all familiar with the ebb and flow of the tides which are caused by the attraction of the sun and in greater measure of the moon. The force required is about one nine millionth part of the earth's attraction and it forms a kind of swelling in the sea which, due to the funnel-like formation in many bays, rises to a height of nine, twelve, or even seventeen metres. At new moon and full moon it causes spring tides and at half moon neap tides depending on whether the sun and moon are in the same direction or opposite directions, or are at right angles with regard to the earth.

These phenomena naturally affect the life of man and nature, particularly in coastal areas. In addition to this daily rhythm of the moon there are connections between its monthly cycle and the biological processes in man. Doctors have experimented with urine and ascertained that the production of uric acid is weakest after the new moon. It increases before and after the last quarter and diminishes again round about full moon. They established a regular rhythm of about 5 periods of 6 days which is clearly connected with the synodial month of 29.5 days, i.e. the time the moon takes to go round the earth.

The same is true of menstruation. Dr. Guthmann wrote an article on it in the *Medical World*. A hundred and four cases were examined and they all showed a great increase in menstruation periods at new and full moon. This is all the more remarkable because sickness, differences in individuals and harmful effects of civilisation all play an important part as well.

These things are not caused by the moonlight. They occur in exactly the same way in curtained rooms where there are sick people. Neither must they be confused with being moonstruck. Doctors say that the same effect can be produced as well by artificial light.

The palolo worm is a widely-known and typical example of the effect of the moon on animals. At the beginning of spring, one day before the last quarter of the moon enormous quantities of palolo worms rise to the surface of the sea for multiplication. They emit a tail twenty to forty cms long for this purpose. The inhabitants of Samoa and other islands look forward to their coming and eat them with relish. The Swedish astronomer and Nobel prize-winner, Svante Arrhenius, solved the riddle of why all these creatures, who live in coral caves deep down in the ocean, are so punctual. He found that the phases of the moon corresponded to variations in the content of electricity in the air. Sea urchins and other creatures are affected in the same way.

The influence of the moon on the growth of plants has long been a matter for dispute. Peasants say that radish seeds should be sown under a waning moon because radishes have to grow downwards; lettuce seeds should be sown under a waxing moon because lettuces grow upwards. This is too simple. It does not take into consideration the fact that leaves and roots must maintain a biological equilibrium all the time. Weak roots give few leaves and vice versa. Again the popular idea is that trees should be planted at full moon because the moon has driven the sap upwards. They should be cut down at new moon because then the sap is still in the roots. The substance of the moon, however, has nothing to do with its luminous form. It is always about the same.

The idea that the moon affects the weather is as old as it is false. Changes of the moon have practically nothing to do with changes in the weather. Everyone can see that for himself. It is surprising that this supposed influence still finds a place in astrological calendars.

The Sun

That the influence of the sun is much greater and affects the life of plants, animals and men hardly needs mention. The Egyptian king Akenaton (c. 1450 B.C.), called it, with justification, "the great giver of blessing".

There are two rhythms in our relationship to the sun: the daily one and the annual one. Our average pulse shows a regular rise and fall, whether we are ill or at work. At twelve o'clock it is about 74, at midnight about 59 according to the meridian. Emigrants adapt themselves very slowly. Within the arctic circle there is the long night of about twenty-four hours which gives a unique rhythm independent of the short day. Our evening temp-

erature is higher than the one in the morning. Mortality is at its
highest between four and six o'clock in the morning, whereas on
an average, the fewest people die every year between seven and
ten o'clock.

The yearly rhythm shows that human receptivity is at its best
in April and May. Mental cases undergo a crisis in the spring. It
is not only a time when poets and birds sing but also when the
number of suicides increases. On the other hand epileptics experience a period of freedom at this time, but they are strongly
affected by variations in the earth's magnetism.

Sun spots certainly play a part in our lives as well as causing
the crackling noises in radio communications over the Atlantic
and similar physical effects. (Diagram 8). Two French doctors in
conjunction with the leader of the meteorological station on Mont
Blanc have proved that sun spots have an effect on the state of
sick people. For 276 days 237 patients in Nice and near Paris

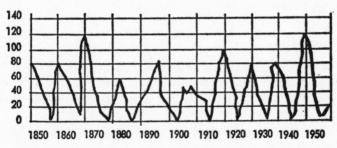

Diag. 8   Relative number of sunspots in each decade.

were observed and findings recorded at the station. These observations were collated with those of the sun spots. The results
showed that eighty-four per cent of the number of large spots
passing through the sun's meridian coincided with unusual signs
of illness. Only thirty-three per cent of the periods when there
were no spots gave a similar result. This was confirmed by the
same doctors after five years of observation.

It is certain that the general level of excitability is increased
during the periods when sun spots are very frequent but it is
very doubtful whether we can attribute the outbreak of wars to
this fact. It is also uncertain whether the planet Jupiter exercises
any influence in this respect. We must bear in mind that its gravi-
tational pull is a hundred times less than the moon's and that is
weak enough.

It is of course possible that the eleven year cycle of sun spots has something to do with the passage of Jupiter round the sun and that this again may affect the growth of trees. In that case we should see not only the effect of dry and wet years on the rings of a fallen tree trunk, but also traces of stellar influence. Biologists like Thomas Ring, who concern themselves with cosmology, point out that the stars may act as catalysts through whose presence changes come about. They refer to the human organism in which the smallest doses can bring about great changes. For example a one four-millionth solution of adrenalin can cause blood pressure to rise.

These are mostly hypotheses, possibilities. In actual fact we have no provable or measurable evidence of the influence of the stars on man, only of the sun and moon. We must be careful to note that everything we have discussed is only the average and general effect on group samples. This does not justify the astrologists' claim to have proved by rule of thumb that the stars shape and alter the character and destiny of the individual. This question requires much more careful thought.

The Principles of Astrology

From the extensive sphere of astrology certain principles can be extracted and submitted to critical examination.

1. Astrology teaches that only the seven planets have any effect on our destiny apart from the sun, the moon, and some 150 stars of the zodiac. Some of the fixed stars are consulted for exact horoscopes.

Here is cause for astonishment. We can see about 2,000 stars in our sky. The Babylonians could see 3,500, about the number that can be seen from the Zugspitze in Germany. Millions of stars, including gigantic suns are known to the astronomer. Over our heads we see the Great Bear, the beautiful constellation of Orion or the bluish light of Vega. Do they have no significance for us? Has our neighbouring sun Sirius, only eight light-years away, no influence? That surely is remarkable! Why do these bright stars have no influence? The astrologers give no reason. They merely say they do not know the reason; it is knowledge that has been handed down to them. Another remarkable thing is that not only stars above the horizon but also those below it are said to exert an influence, which therefore penetrates the 12,000 km of the earth's diameter. No one has ever observed these rays or their effect. Gravity is a physical quantity and has no quality that could alter our character or destiny.

2. The second principle seems equally doubtful. It is not the

stars I can see that measure my life, but those which were visible at the time of my birth. My horoscope is decisive for my whole life, which like a stone thrown into the water extends its ripples further and further.

This is traceable to a very old belief from earliest times. The beginning decides the continuation (see Chapter 1). Of course everybody, apart from a certain vital freedom of the will, is conditioned by parents and grandparents. We know too the Mendelian laws of heredity. But these laws can be demonstrated, whereas the idea that the moment of birth stamps your whole life is very doubtful, if only from the fact that it is not certain what is meant by birth. Does it occur when the first breath is drawn or when the umbilical cord is cut? The astrologers themselves are not certain on this point. At the moment of conception a new being is created and the characteristics of the child have been decided by the genes long before actual birth. The moment of conception however is never definite; it remains a secret within the mother's body. If the rays penetrate through the whole earth, why not into the thin covering of a mother's body? One question leads to another.

Then take the case of twins. As their horoscopes are alike they would have to remain alike for their whole lives. In fact some twins do have a similar destiny and similar gifts and inclinations. But there are examples of quintuplets two of whom die and three survive; of one twin living to eighty years of age when the other was killed in the war when he was twenty. That is inexplicable if the horoscopes are decisive.

Besides twins in body there are twins in horoscope. On an average 240 children are born at the same time. Goethe, Napoleon and Beethoven had plenty of horoscope twins, but none of them achieved the same fame as poet, general or composer. If one finds that one became Emperor of the French while another took a leading part in a rabbit club, that proves that there must be other factors which determine the future of people. When an astrologer asserts that according to his horoscope, Rilke had to be a lyric poet, why have we not heard of the 200 other lyric poets who were born under the same stars?

In order to understand this second principle we should of course have to know why the astrologers make these assertions. If we depended on the stars we can see today, we should all suffer the same fate; e.g. we should all be in danger from the traffic together with the some five millions of people who live on the same meridian. You can only give an individual answer when you take the person's moment of birth and satisfy the curiosity and anxiety of someone who wants to know his particular fate today or tomorrow.

3. The third principle derives the working of the stars from the meaning of the names given to them by the Babylonians or the Greeks, or the names given by the astronomers to newly discovered stars. This sounds surprising at first, but in actual fact the name given in late Greek times, though differing from a former name, was supposed to correspond exactly with the effect of the star. The Greek and Roman goddess of love, Venus, was said to create beautiful men and women with round, shining eyes and pretty faces, with long luxuriant hair (especially the women) and with an inclination for pleasure and sensuous desires. The astrologer Frickler describes her in the following verse:

> To Venus beauty, harmony,
> Music-making melody,
> Radiance and fantasy,
> And fragrant robe the god hath lent;
> Symphony replete with love
> She doth send caressingly.
> And she gives at every kiss
> To every lover her own bliss.

She is the star of artists, hair stylists, goldsmiths, jewellers, cooks, hosts, dancers, hunters, maidens and match-makers.

Because Saturn was the oldest god, the father of Jupiter, who ate his children in order to have no descendants, men born under this planet are solemn, tough, gloomy, slow, and cunning. In the Middle Ages they were described as:

> Hairy, strong and limping old;
> Stinking, half-deformed and cold,
> Thus am I; my progeny
> Will ever after live like me.

The astrologers aver that the erotic effect does not come because the star is called Venus, but the star was called Venus because of its erotic influence. In answer to that, one may well ask why the planet Neptune, discovered in 1846 by Galle and Lavoisier was immediately named Lord of the Fish and was supposed to have caused the loss of the Titanic in 1912? Had there been, before then, any such cases?

In the year 1930 a boy discovered quite by chance a small planet circling at a great distance. Lowell had been making theoretical calculations of its existence for some time before. The astronomers gave it the name of Pluto. Not even one eighth of its course could be observed but the astrologers soon decided it was a dangerous being, even worse than Mars. It is the planet of motor cars and earthquakes. This was because in Greek legend, Pluto was the god of the underworld.

Even wrong observations are used for interpretation. All primitive peoples associated the moon with water because cloudless nights were very dewy. In reality dew is formed by the cooling of the atmosphere and the moon has nothing to do with it.

How deeply this idea is rooted in people's minds is indicated by the word "influence". It was thought originally that fluid "flowed" to and from the moon. The reddish colour of Mars was supposed to show his bloodthirsty and fiery character. In reality we should have to put on very warm clothes if we wanted to take a walk on it. It is considerably colder than the earth.

A third false notion is added to this belief in names or rather fetish of names. It is an arid schematisation. The signs of the zodiac are divided into masculine and feminine ones. This was not done with any serious thought or from observed effects but by alternate repetition such as children delight in. The resultant consequences were devoid of sense. For example, Ptolemaeus thought that if a man had Venus in his sign of the zodiac he would be a homosexual and shamefully weak, giving himself up to infamy. Since, however, Venus on an average stays one month in each sign, it would mean that half the men and women were homosexual. What has become of the ancient wisdom of the stars? Is not Wilhelm Gundels, a sympathetic authority on the history of astrology, right when he calls it "stereotyped work"?

4. The fourth principle concerns the teaching of the so-called "aspects". According to this, an uninterrupted influence passes from the star or planet to the individual. Much depends on the angle formed by the rays from the constellation and the birthplace, or more exactly the body of the person concerned. Mars for example, is not "pure" Mars. Its influence changes according to the angle the Venus rays form with it.

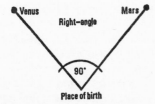

Diag. 9
False representation of the rays from the planets.

134

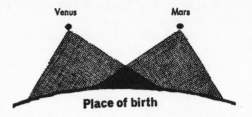

Venus   Mars

Diag. 10
Correct representation of
the rays from the planets.   **Place of birth**

This idea is devoid of rational content. How can a qualitative change in character or destiny be brought about by a purely geometrical function? Does this whole conception have any connection with reality? Are not these rays which go out in all directions broken up a millionfold by the rays from other stars before they get as far as man? (diagrams 9-10).

When we look at a horoscope we notice that, according to astrology, each of the ten planets, which include the sun and moon, covers sixteen main aspects; i.e. 160 points of effectiveness altogether. As the astrologer reckons not only with the exact angle but also with the so-called *orbis* which gives a play of from two to five degrees, every point of the horoscope has three or four aspects. In other words there are so many possible interpretations that all hope of certitude slips from our grasp. Aspects can prove anything or nothing. The Swiss astrologer Frankhauser admitted that this multiplication had called forth justifiable criticism and scorn. "You can be sure," he wrote, "of hitting a mouse if you fire 500 shells into a square metre! And with 160 possible places for aspects in the horoscope you are bound to find some explanation."

5. Let us turn to the fifth principle. Apart from aspects, there is no pure ray from a planet. Its influence will be modified by the sign of the zodiac in which it stands. Therefore an important element in drawing up a horoscope is the "ascendent", by which is meant the planet or sign of the zodiac which is rising exactly in the east at the time of the birth.

Let us take a closer look at these signs of the zodiac, these interesting constellations and their legends.

In the course of a year the sun appears to pass over the twelve signs. This track or "heavenly highway", as the Babylonians named it, is called the ecliptic. This means the road of extinction or eclipse of the sun and moon. In reality it is brought about by the intervention of the earth. We circle the sun every year and in the background ever fresh constellations appear moving in the same. direction. The Babylonians reckoned with a system of twelve, so they found twelve constellations. We could equally well find ten or fourteen.

The names of the signs arose in a very natural way. The spring sign, the Ram, for example, was called the hireling, Sumerian *hun-gar*, Babylonian *a-gru*, because in spring the landowner hired labourers. In April and May the cows were covered by the bulls. June was not the time of the twins. The constellation was conceived as a married couple. This was the time for marriages! The harvest sign was an ear of corn. It was only later put into the hand of a virgin. In summer the great kings went hunting the lion, hence the sign of that name. The sign in which the sun seemed to be losing its strength and departing was called the crab, and the scales were a good representation of the autumnal equinox. The Babylonian winter had three rainy months, so these signs were called Capricorn, Aquarius and Pisces. The Capricorn was a goat with a fish's tail.

As the Greeks did not hire labourers in spring they called the sign the Ram because it was lambing time. In our January they hunted the wild goat but they did not know of the capricorn.

From this we can see how naturally the names arose without the aid of a "third" eye, a kind of parietal, primitive eye which, according to Professor Dacqué of Munich, must have existed at one time. The names are not universal either, and interpretations differ from one country to another. For the Mayas, Venus was a bringer of ill-luck. When her star appeared in the sky, they blocked up the chimneys so as to keep harm away. In Babylonia Saturn was a prophet of good tidings.

Among the Chinese everything is again different. In their paper *The Stars and Man* astrologers admit this. Aquarius, sign of the intellectuals, becomes the rat, and the fish turns into a pig!

But let us look at the stars as they really are. It is said that Venus rides on the bull or she rules the bull or she is in the house of the bull. That is all nonsense. The individual stars of a constellation have often no connection with each other. They only appear from our point of view to be in the same direction. This can be seen with the beautiful constellation of the plough. Its stars belong to different groups and star drifts and are moving away from each other. In 50,000 or even 10,000 years' time we shall not see it any more, at least not in its present form (Diagram 11). Its stars are between 80 and 200 light-years away and a nebula that seems to be in the plough is 150 million light-years away. The word "in" is misleading, as misleading as if I put a pin to my eye, looked in the direction of Frankfurt and said the

136

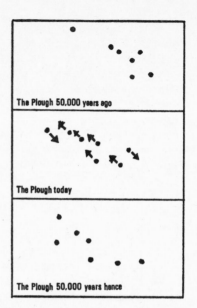

The Plough 50,000 years ago

The Plough today

Diag. 11
The arrows show the direction in which
each star is travelling.

The Plough 50,000 years hence

town was in the pin. The same thing is true of the Lion. Its chief
star, Regulus, is 79 light-years away. Epsilon, another of its stars,
is 1,630 light-years away. They have no possible connection. Pictorial representation of constellations belongs to the world of the
Babylonians. For them all the stars were fixed on a solid hemisphere, hence the term fixed star, and all were equidistant from
the earth. Modern knowledge has put these conceptions out of
date.

The great weakness of astrology is that it confines itself to the
northern hemisphere, which the Babylonians also did. With us
the sun is in the sign of the Lion in summer and is at its hottest.
At the same time it is winter in the southern hemisphere. It is
therefore contrary to reason to establish a close connection between the sun, heat and the Lion.

In the opinion of serious astrologers like R. Ebertins of Aalen,
the current idea of being a *fish-man* or a *bull-man* is only true
to a limited extent. This description envisages only one part of a
man's being, namely his relationship to the sun. Astrologers regard the ascendents as more important. According to them the
ascendent, i.e. the star rising exactly in the east at the moment of
birth is what really forms the personality and it is precisely
this which is overlooked in the weekly horoscopes published in
newspapers and periodicals. Even the publisher of the *Lorch
Astrological Calendar* queries whether they are playing fair with
the public.

Astronomy gives a further ground for reducing the readings from the signs of the zodiac to absurdity. It concerns the apparent *precession* of the sun. The idea arises from the fact that the earth completes one revolution of its axis in about 26,000 years. Because of this the sun's spring position moves slowly through the zodiac, so that today the sun is no longer in the Ram but in the fish at the spring equinox and will soon be in Aquarius. So all *Ram-men* would now be really *Fish-men* if the astrologers had not found an astonishing way out of the difficulty. They maintain that radiation does not proceed from the present-day stars but from those which were apparent 4,000 years ago, i.e. at the time when they were given names, and the laws which governed them were discovered. We must therefore draw a sharp distinction between *signs* and *constellations*. The latter are simply designations for the first to the thirtieth degree, from the thirtieth to the sixtieth degree and so on. Astronomers will understand this distinction clearly.

Those who do not find these facts convincing should remember that psychological research knows nothing of these twelve types of people nor of the idea that men's character and destiny change from one month of birth to another. In his *Constitutional Psychology*, Kreschmer distinguishes certain exact types after conducting a detailed investigation of 80,000 people. The three main types were found to be distributed equally through all the months of the year.

Before going on to discover what there is of sense and nonsense in horoscopes, there are two further principles to be seen.

6. The sixth principle. The meaning of the planets, aspects and signs of the zodiac are further modified through their dependence on the twelve *houses of life* which change every two hours according to the revolution of the earth on its axis. One may well ask why these houses were invented. What were formerly elements in the horoscope now change so slowly that most people would have the same fate. The sun, Mercury and Venus remain in one sign for about a month; Mars for about two months; Jupiter for a year; Saturn two and a half years, Uranus seven years, Neptune fourteen and Pluto more than twenty. Only the moon is in a hurry. It passes through a sign in two and a half days or, to be more exact, 13.5 per cent in twenty-four hours. People born in the same year have five planets in the same sign, so both their character and their destiny should be the same, but this runs contrary to all experience.

When anyone seeks astrological advice it is usually about a particular question. The business man wants to know whether he

138

should start a new advertising campaign in the next month. A young girl wants to know whether her lover will be faithful. If the significance of the sign in a birth horoscope changes every two hours, I can give excellent advice. Indeed the houses, not to be confused with the signs of the zodiac, give a clear classification suited to the enquirer: it depends on your personality, finances, brothers and sisters, father, children, health, wife, death, journeys, religion, profession, friends and enemies!

There are differences between the houses. The first, fourth, seventh, and tenth are known as *corner* or *cardinal* houses; the second, fifth, eighth and eleventh, *successive* and the third, sixth, ninth and twelfth are called *falling*. In Schiller's *Wallenstein*, Seni, the astrologer, prophesies fresh good fortune shortly before Wallenstein's violent assassination. "Saturn is harmless," he says, "powerless in the falling house".

The astrologers do not give us any rational explanation of anything to do with the stars. Even Kepler was against much of their teaching, and besides, the astrologers are not all of one mind. For example, there are four utterly contradictory principles for classifying the houses. Some time ago I corresponded with a well-known astrologer. He wrote to say that I should need to be educated scientifically and be able to read horoscopes before I could correspond with him. I replied that I had already worked out dozens of horoscopes but should like to learn more about the science of it. I asked him which classification of the houses he thought was the right one: Campanus' (*c.* 1300), Regiomontanus' (*c.* 1450), Placidus' (*c.* 1650) or the modern method of equalising the houses. He did not reply. This man had foretold a thunderstorm in a Swabian town. Even towns consult astrologers to make sure an open air fête will not be spoilt by rain. On this occasion it did actually thunder on a Sunday in July as he had prophesied and he grumbled because he had only been paid ten marks for it. As he had reckoned that the storm must take place because of a recession of Neptune and had made other successful forecasts, he thought he deserved not ten marks but a Nobel prize, for he claimed to have put Copernicus in the shade!

After the consideration of one last principle—the seventh—we shall have sufficient knowledge to be able to form a judgment.

7. The horoscope is said to embrace not only a man's character but his whole future life. How does one know all the coming events? There is nothing simpler. You see them from the so-called "Directions" and "Transits".

Neither the teachers of the ancient wisdom nor the Babylonians had yet discovered this amazing method of forecasting. They were content to look only a year ahead. The Greek scholars of the late Alexandrine period were the first to make any forecasts for ten, twenty or eighty years ahead and the medieval astrologers followed suit. The primary directions state that the first four minutes of life determine the first year; the fifth to the eighth minute the second year and so on. In four minutes the sky appears to turn through one degree, fifteen in one hour and fifteen by twenty-four equals 360 degrees.

If therefore Mr. Red and Miss Blue get to know each other and fall in love, and if he marries her in his twenty-fourth year he does not need to look up at the stars that are shining at the time. The stars that were visible at the ninety-sixth minute of his life, i.e. about an hour and a half after his birth, had already brought about the marriage. In this case the stars work like a kind of time fuse. A conjunction of Mars and Venus in the eightieth minute of life produces a love affair when the individual is twenty. As the wheel of the horoscope can be turned indefinitely it is possible to calculate our love affairs at the age of ninety or a hundred and twenty!

There is also a quite different method for calculating the future. According to this *key*, twenty-four hours, not four minutes, represents a year. Thus the position of the stars on the twentieth day represents what will happen in the twentieth year. The astrologers make no attempt to explain the variations or coordinate these two methods. Sometimes they use one, sometimes the other, and in the standard textbook on the subject other methods, including the transit method, are recommended.

By a transit is meant the time when the present sun crosses the place in the sky it occupied at the time of your birth. Such a spot exists only on paper. Our whole solar system is moving forward at the great speed of twenty km a second or 72,000 km an hour. This amounts to nearly a milliard km a year. Our place in the stars is the nebula of Orion which the naked eye sees as a tiny cloud, and we are being rushed at break-neck speed towards the constellation of Hercules; but we need have no fear; there will be no collision. There is no such crush in the sky as prevails in our parking places!

We are now in a position to study two examples of a horoscope.

First Horoscope (Diagram 12)

This horoscope shows Scorpion in the ascendent. According to Brandler-Pracht, the Grand Old Man of astrology, such people are

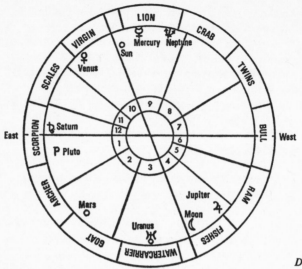

Diag. 12

mostly phlegmatic and taciturn. This does not prevent him from
asserting the opposite, ten lines later. He says that such people
are also very talkative and make good speakers. In all cases they
go to excess and exercise a disintegrating influence. They are
very fond of arms and like everything to do with aquatics and
seafaring.

The ascendent is in close conjunction with Saturn and forms a
right angle with Uranus. This means a life overshadowed by misfortune. There is also a threat of illness: constipation, stones
in the kidneys or the bladder, drying up of the joint capsules,
knee trouble and rheumatism. Uranus it is true has a favourable
effect on the aura, the od, the flesh of the scalp and the spinal
cord, and secondarily on the calves and the bones of the foot,
but other astrologers say this rectangle indicates syphilis. The
misfortune is heightened because Pluto, king of the underworld, is
in the first house.

The sun and moon being in opposition is also an unfavourable
sign. It foretells bad health, a threat to one's honour, lack of
popularity and inebriety. Another important aspect is Jupiter in
opposition to Venus. It means that the unfortunate wretch has
nothing to hope for in love or art. Furthermore his love of dis-
play will ruin him.

Even so there are glimmers of light in this horoscope of gloom.
The sun high in the sky promises success and prestige. Neptune
is also well placed and combined with the strength of Mars points

to his becoming a sailor. But Saturn and Pluto are upsetting, so that drowning seems to be this man's fate.

In order to learn more it is advisable to read what the writers of antiquity have to say. Franz Boll has taken a lot of trouble to do this. Theukros Rhetorios tells us that when Scorpion is in the ascendent it means a black skin and woolly hair. According to Antiochos the sun and moon in opposition indicates epileptics and people possessed by an evil spirit, and the great Roman astrologer, Firmus Maternus says outright that those who are born under the eighteenth degree of Scorpion will be torn to pieces by wild beasts.

Now we can name the date of birth of this epileptic negro or drunken sailor. It is August 28th, 1749, and the place of birth, Frankfurt-on-Main. It is Goethe's horoscope! Is this not a striking proof of the arbitrariness and wild imagination that underlie the rules of astrology? Of course if the astrologer knows whose horoscope he has before him, it is not difficult to select out of the many possibilities the appropriate interpretations. That may be the case with the horoscope which Louisa Rinser ordered for Theresa of Konnersreuth from a famous astrologer.

Let us look at another one.

In order to give the secret away at once, this is Hitler's horoscope. What picture of his life does astrology draw? We learn the following indications: The sun in opposition to the ascendent points to ill-health affecting particularly the eyes and the brain. The moon in conjunction with Jupiter points to success and powerful friends. He will be noble-minded and beneficent. The moon in the fourth house means a happy home life and a care-free old age; the sun in the seventh house shows a radiant marriage and a good family life. The planet Mars is wiped out by the Bull. This betokens a peaceful gentleman farmer and a great dislike of war. Saturn in the tenth house gives the qualities needed for trades such as coal merchant, shoemaker, printer, night watchman and sexton, also farm worker. The Sun in triple relationship to the Moon and Jupiter promises a happy constellation for party and people. Finally Neptune in the eighth house indicates a glorious death far away. This is why many astrologers think that Hitler is still alive and may be in hiding in South America.

As this horoscope does not altogether fit in with the facts, one astrologer has suggested that the date of birth is wrong. It belongs to an ordinary citizen of Braunau or Dingskirchen and he thinks Hitler used the papers of his insignificant brother.

In fairness it must be said that another astrologer foretold a rise to power and a sudden fall, especially with Saturn in the tenth house. In spite of this he was one of the enthusiastic people who prepared the way for Hitler in 1933-4. In his paper, *The New Germany*, he wrote: "Fear of the Brownshirts is unfounded, because they will follow the orders of the Führer with the strictest discipline and without hesitation. There is no danger of bloodshed or illegal practices, as certain short-sighted party papers have described." In the same paper he said there would be a new world currency not based on gold in 1933-4 and there would also be a great increase in the German Communist Party. A new economy based on justice would be introduced. Schleicher, Brüning and Ehrhardt would play a major part in the government. Russia was on the verge of a revolution which would be fatal for Stalin. If war broke out the masses would rise in revolt against him.

So said the astrologers and thereby strengthened the rulers in their madness and contributed to the ruin of the German people. One of them, C. H. Huter, stated at that time that according to his horoscope Hitler's party was unbreakable.

The Age of Aquarius, Stellar Medicine and Political Astrology

As we have seen, all the constellations viewed from this planet are apparently being gradually shifted with regard to their position relative to the sun by the sun's so-called precession. The constellations no longer correspond to the signs. In astrology the Lion means the lion's strength which emanated from that constellation at the place of its appearance four thousand years ago when viewed from the earth.

This distinction applies to the whole question of the interpretation of the stars. There is, however, one important exception. We are told again and again about the coming Aquarian age and this refers to the sign of the zodiac. In recent times the sun has been in this sign on March 21st, the advent of spring.

During the last two thousand years the prevailing sign was thought to be the Fish. It marked the Christian era in which the virtues of piety, beneficence and love of one's neighbour had been practised and had made man modest and humble. Now, after many transitional struggles, a better and more beautiful age is coming—the Aquarian age. It marks the dawn of a world republic. Man will become a creature of light. He will travel in space ships to new planets. Peace and happiness will reign everywhere!

Whereas Christ has been the new Messiah for the past two thousand years, no new Messiahs have been found for the Aquarian age. In a private letter circulated to the initiated it said, "A new Son of God will arise who will wear the sun on his countenance. He will end the age of Christ and be the teacher of the future world. This herald of wisdom and new Messiah is Carl Huter who was born in 1861 on October 9th, at the beginning of the new epoch. He will enlighten us about the meaning and purpose of our lives and usher in a new social order and bring new knowledge of God."

Carl Huter was the father of C. H. Huter, the owner of an astrological publishing house in Stuttgart. He publishes a calendar with a *red* cover while his former wife, who runs a similar business in Munich, advertises widely in her *blue* calendar. It is hardly credible that hundreds of thousands of people read such productions and even believe what they say.

One cannot call the last two thousand years an age of true Christianity. There are many peoples who have not yet heard of it and all Christian missions are banned for the 600 million Chinese. Christ's words are still valid: "Go ye into all the world and make disciples of all the nations."

But even if this were not the case, the rest of astrology would still be in disagreement, for it connects the power of the stars not with their actual position but with their signs. Anyone who talks about the Fish age or the Aquarian age has thereby tacitly admitted that every horoscope is wrong. I keep an open mind and am ready to admit the irrational as well as the rational, but in this matter I can only say that astrologers do not take truth seriously. They are either deceiving themselves or deceiving other people.

The same thing applies to what is called *stellar medicine*. It simplifies diagnosis by making one part of the body correspond to one of the signs of the zodiac. The Ram is the head, the Bull the neck, the Twins the arms and breast, the Crab the abdomen etc. Whichever sign you happen to be born under endangers that part of the body. Here again the astrologers are not all of one mind. Boll points out that there are numerous and often contradictory systems of astrological medicine. The above division, however, is accepted by the majority.

The planets can also affect particular organs and functions of the body by their *radiations*. For example, the sun has an effect on the circulation of the blood and the cell structures. The moon affects the blood serum, lymph and the cerebellum. Jupiter has quite a complicated task. He controls the sugar content of the liver and if he is in an unfavourable position he can bring on corpulence. Neptune also has an unenviable task. According to Brandler-Pracht he exerts an influence on the brain, the eyes, the feet, the toes and the appendix. He is also responsible for deafness and when in an unfavourable position causes lethargy, hallucination and other mental disturbances.

Diagnosis of illness therefore becomes easy. You can do it from any distance. With the patient's horoscope before you, you do not need to see him. The cure is equally clever. A distinguished Arab astrologer recommends the following cure for all the dreaded forms of cancer: "When the sun and moon are in the sign of the Crab, catch crabs, boil them, grind to a powder and then rub it on the cancerous places." If this were so, hospitals would not need to spend large sums on cobalt X-ray apparatus. Astrologers will cure the disease more cheaply. In the Middle Ages, these rules of astrology were important for the widespread practice of letting blood. The artery was cut at the place designated by the sign of the zodiac in the ascendent at the time.

One small tip for those who are afraid of losing their hair. Only go to the barber when the moon is full. Their locks will then grow in luxuriant abundance!

Political astrology needs only a passing mention. Horoscopes can be drawn up for countries, towns and villages as well as for individuals. They also have their rulers among the stars who can influence them for good or ill. The Twins rule the United States. The Lion presides over France and Italy. Ptolemaeus apportioned the Ram to England and Germany. He also gives his reason. The English and the Germans are as stubborn as the Ram!

The kindly, equable sign of the Scales presides over the towns of Heilbronn, Halle, Wimpfen, Ludwigsburg, Lisbon and Rio de Janeiro. The revolutionary Scorpion influences towns like Munich, Geneva, Liverpool, Washington, Wildbad and Tübingen. How do the astrologers know all this? By the ancient rule: how it begins, so it goes on, i.e. from the particular town's horoscope. The fate of the German Empire can be calculated from January 18th, 1871, at 12.15 p.m. when Bismarck read the proclamation of the Emperor. Historians would indeed be grateful if the stars would tell them the exact date of the founding of towns and empires, for astrologers claim to reckon backwards in time.

You would have thought that every rational being would have detected the nonsense in all this by now; yet astrological calendars and periodicals are still widely read and you often come across the horoscope of the United States or the Soviet Union promulgated by the most reputable astrologers.

Criticism

When such illogical reasonings are pointed out to believers in the stars, they reply, "that may be so, but experience justifies us over and over again," and they quote cases of successful character-forecasting. What are we to think? Let me here offer some examples of absolute failures. They could be multiplied many times over.

We might begin with Kepler who lived at the time of the Thirty Years' War. His famous horoscope of Wallenstein has been regarded as a show piece by astrologers. Yet it proved thoroughly false. He said Wallenstein would marry at thirty-three. He married at twenty-six and forty. Kepler said he would increase in esteem, authority and possessions in his years from forty-seven to fifty-two. Wallenstein was dismissed in his forty-seventh year, restored a year and a half later and murdered when he was fifty-one. Kepler had foretold that he would die from fever in his seventieth year. This horoscope was made in 1608. Sixteen years later, Wallenstein asked for a corrected one as the first one had been incorrect in certain details. But the corrected version proved equally false. It indicated a period of good fortune from 1630 on and no particular danger for the year of his assassination (1634). Furthermore Kepler already knew his client before the horoscope was made.

In his own family Kepler was also unfortunate with his forecasts. He said his eldest son would have long life and become a prince. The sorrowing parents buried the child when he was only a year and a half old.

I have before me a copy of the genuine *Hundred Years Calendar* published about 1650 by the Abbé Mauritius Knauer and now republished on account of its historical curiosity. The abbé thought the seven planets ruled the weather, which therefore recurred every seven years. The calendar was given its name by a smart bookseller in Erfurt in the year 1721 and it is still believed in today. In February 1956, for example, we had the coldest weather for many years and it lasted several weeks. This calendar said there would be downpours of rain and it would remain wet from February 12th to the end of the month; the winter would be warm and wet!

Modern calendar makers completely failed to foretell the winter of 1962/3, which was the coldest for half a century. Writing, not according to the *Hundred Years Calendar*, but according to his own reckoning, the editor of the *Lorch Astrological Calendar* says, "There will be a normal winter for 1962/3 with many storms and some warm periods." He recommended sowing seeds on March 4th and 5th. On these days, the temperature in South Germany fell to ten to twenty degrees centigrade below freezing and the ground was covered in ice and snow.

The same miscalculations occur in forecasting serious accidents. Although every month is to have its toll of accidents on the roads and in the air, and important people will die, the Lorch Calendar also prophesies for December 4th, 1959, "Windy. Good for visiting, travelling and official business in the afternoon," and in black type, *"The month begins with a favourable influence."* On this date the floods in Fréjus on the Mediterranean coast cost 320 lives.

The eclipse of the sun on February 4th, 1962, aroused great fear throughout the world. Indian astrologers prophesied the end of the world. Terrified crowds prayed for hours in the open air. The *Lorch Astrological Calendar* announced that the total eclipse of the sun would cause terrible catastrophes, revolutions, wars and even changes in the earth's surface. Europe would, of course, be involved in the suffering, but this time the worst effects would be felt in the far east.

In reality nothing exceptional happened in India at the time, nor in any other Asian countries. There were, it is true, the disastrous floods in Hamburg on February 16th and 17th. According to the astrologers, this town, being a port, comes under the influence of Aquarius. Catastrophes were forecast from February 4th, but between then and the 16th is too great a length of time for there to be any connection. In such calendars there are numerous prophecies of disasters, so some are bound to fit in.

Let us now look at a few examples where the forecast was completely false. For the end of September and the month of October, 1959, sharp differences were to arise between America and Russia. At this time General Eisenhower and Mr. Khrushchev were having friendly talks in Camp David. Khrushchev's horoscope said his position would weaken in the summer, whereas it grew stronger. In October and November America was to make good progress towards reaching the moon. The newspapers reported failures.

Astrologers were also wrong about the oubreak of the Second World War. An English astrologer named Lyndor, wrote on August 13th, 1939, "Anyone who thinks there will be war at the end of the month is past praying for." And again on August 27th, "Hitler will never do it." Another English astrologer named Naylor, wrote in the *Sunday Express*, two days before the war started, "Hitler's horoscope is not a warlike one. If war comes, not he but others will strike the first blow."

In 1925 a criminal named Haarmann was executed for committing thirty murders. The astrologer he had consulted prophesied much happiness for him in 1950 and 1954. He described the man's character in these words. "Benevolent, thoughtful, peaceable with a sound outlook on life, witty, humorous, good-hearted and with a fine sense of sympathy."

It is interesting to inquire why many forecasts turn out right in spite of their logical impossibility. The answer is not difficult.

1. In 1552, Luther pointed out in his *Table Talk* that the astrologers attribute successes to their own judgment and are wise enough to keep silent about their failures.

Luther's remark applies equally to today. In the course of their three thousand years' history astrologers have never produced any useful statistics or series of proofs though we gladly acknowledge the efforts made by Krafft and H. von Klöckler. The latest attempts that have been made to draw up any that can be regarded as scientific have been made by a Frenchman, Michel Guackelin. As far as traditional astrology is concerned, the results are purely negative. More research is needed before we can be sure that the definite connections he makes between the date of birth and the choice of a career are valid.

2. Knowledge of human nature and wide experience can do much, especially when joined to skill in questioning a client. All kinds of aids to diagnosis can be drawn out of him or her, as was seen with clairvoyance.

3. General and ambiguous statements are made. The oracle at Delphi relied largely on such ambiguities.

4. People are often deceived about themselves. "You are intelligent," "You are loyal to your friends," we should all like to have these things said about us. "You often feel well, often relaxed." "Be careful about catching cold in December!" Such statements do not need any knowledge of the stars.

5. One last quite different reason. Many astrologers are telepathic. They possess great sensitiveness and powers of sympathy. The horoscope stimulates them in the same way that coffee, playing cards or pendulum divining does others. It awakens activity in their subconscious mind. There is nothing firm or tangible about this gift, as we saw when talking about clairvoyance. All clairvoyants are often subject to error, and no one

can rely on the faint possibility that the astrologer possesses such a gift. Even so he may be right. Chance also comes into it.

What Christianity Says

Criticism based on experience alone is not enough. We must show what great dangers for faith and man's outlook on the world arise from a belief in the stars. For most of its adherents, astrology is a substitute for religion, and whether they will or not, it drives them further and further away from a moral concept of the world and, in so far as they were Christians before, from all Christian belief.

1. Engaging in astrology sooner or later leads to fatalism. If the hour of our birth determines our whole life, then we can do nothing about it. What will be, will be. Instead of applying ourselves with mind and will to our profession and duties, we consult the book of oracles and put off until tomorrow what we ought to do today. Wallenstein is a good example of this. What is the use of a general who trusts to the stars? He would have done better to have studied the roads leading out of Eger where he was assassinated! But there are still people to be met with who allow themselves to be spellbound by what astrologers say.

I once procured a good job in a factory for a woman refugee. Soon afterwards I met her in the street. "How is it you are not at work?" I asked. She replied, "My astrologer says I am a twin and twins find it difficult to make up their minds. I have noticed that myself, so I have stayed away." When astrologers assert that the stars do not compel, but only incline us to do something they are being evasive.

2. Astrology also leads to hedonism, i.e. seeking primarily happiness and good fortune instead of doing one's duty and obeying the moral laws. If we read the astrological textbooks, we find the things they mostly treat of are success in work, financial gain, winning a lottery and happiness in love. We have already referred to articles on "What sort of women can be seduced?" and "How can I become irresistible with women?"

A lecture given in Stuttgart showed me how cynical astrologers can become in the advice they give to people. After a glance at a young man's date of birth, the lecturer said, "You must go abroad. You will only succeed there." Such advice often sets men on an entirely wrong course and awakens misleading desires. It might have been better for this young man to stay at home and study, or he may have had old parents who needed looking after. Such astrologers are misleaders rather than leaders of souls. A real pastor takes much more trouble with a young man who consults him about his future. Only after much careful thought does he give him any advice, even though he may have known the young man for a long time. We are not here to decide primarily what we want but what our sense of responsibility prompts. An unnecessary change of job, marriage quarrels, financial losses through speculation, these are some of the evil results of listening to astrologers.

I gladly admit that a very few serious-minded and cultured astrologers see and fear these dangers. Dr. W. Koch says: "What the investigator most wants—a fixed time for the events—is the last consideration." W. Kappich puts it more strongly: "All foretelling of the future is an intrusion into the divine order of the world." Indeed he then feels compelled "to reject most of traditional astrology". The pity is that such voices get so small a hearing in the astrological press.

3. *The Jews are the only people in the world who have rejected astrology from the start.* In the Book of Leviticus, chapter 19, verse 31, they are warned: "Regard not them that have familiar spirits, neither seek after wizards to be defiled by them. I am the Lord your God."

Interpretation of the stars is not rejected here because it is unreasonable, nor is it denied that the interpreter may sometimes be right. The reason the *Bible* gives is much deeper. It is based on God's absolute lordship over our lives and His absolute freedom. Those who want to know the future are trying to be master of their own fate and see behind the scenes of God's government of the world. Astrology, however restrained and well-informed, mostly becomes mere soothsaying. The prophet Deutero-Isaiah, who praises God as the Lord of history, lived in the heart of the Babylonian world. In the very holy of holies of astrology he cried incisively: "Let now the astrologers and the star-gazers, the monthly prognosticators stand up and save thee from these things that shall come upon thee. Behold they shall be as stubble; they shall not deliver themselves from the power of the flame" (Isa. 47: 13 f.).

That is the clear position taken up by the Bible. It is here also in line with sound sense and science. The story of the wise men, which has often been quoted as an example to the contrary, even by Christians, really points to the same position. Matthew wants to show that even heathens who believed in the stars could have a presentiment of the coming of a Saviour when the chosen people did not. But they looked for the child in Jerusalem and at the court of the inhuman king Herod. Only the Scriptures could guide them to the small village of Bethlehem and to the crib. The purpose of this story is to direct people away from the stars and towards Christ, not vice versa. This also agrees with Paul's plain words to the Galatians: "But now after that ye have known God, or rather are known of God, how turn ye again to the weak and beggarly elements whereunto ye desire again to be in bondage?"

For the Christian there must be no toying with it, no compromise. This is far from being mere rationalism. We have already pointed out the mysterious connections that exist between man and the earth and the cosmos; but the irrational must never become the anti-rational, otherwise we shall lose ourselves in fanaticism and speculation. Believers in the stars are often egocentric and are slaves to superstitious fears. Let us help them to find a joyous faith and know the kindness of God the Father and Him who, above all the brilliance of the stars, holds the planets in His hand (Rev. 1: 16), the true Morning Star (Rev. 22: 16), and know Christ the Light of the world. We need no table of the stars to reckon by. God has already planned the best for us!

11

The Language of the Hands

FORTUNE-TELLERS, soothsayers, pendulum diviners and astrologers are not the only people who advertise their secret powers. Many people today go to palmists to have their fortunes told. There is an old saying which runs: "Your fortune, life and love are written in your hands." What attitude are we to adopt towards palmistry?

We are here dealing with a perfect example of a *confusion of truth and falsehood*. That there is a correspondence between the body and the soul, between bodily form and quality of character, is true. The wild notions and superstitious speculations connected with it are false. A third aspect of the problem is that abnormal powers of second sight and telepathy also come into it.

Since the time of C. G. Carus we have learnt more about human character. It shows that man is a unified organism. Body and soul are two aspects of the same person. Every part of our body bears some relationship to our character and inherited qualities. The way we walk or bear ourselves betrays something of our personality. An early work on human features and their ability to express character has been attributed to Aristotle. The Romans had a saying *ex ungue leonem*, by which they rightly meant that a lion can be recognised by his claws. An expert in human nature can read the whole man from the way he laughs or makes a remark. The living body is the appearance of the soul, and the soul is the *raison d'être* of the living body.

The hands, as well as the face, have an expressive language of their own which is all the more reliable because the hands cannot lie as the face may sometimes do. Everyone can distinguish the delicate hand of the scholar from the horny hand of the farm worker, the slender fingers of a young woman from the fat fists of a boxer. In the plastic arts we have wonderful examples of how the hands can express the whole man. We have only to think of Dürer's hands of the praying apostle or of Grünewald's picture of the crucifixion with Mary Magdalene's hands joined in agony. Michelangelo made many drawings of hands. So did

Rodin. One thinks too of the hands in Titian's picture of the tribute money.

It is not only the shape of the hands that speaks; their movements and gestures are even more eloquent and revealing. The clenched fist of an angry man threatening someone, the warning forefinger of the teacher, the loving, outstretched hands of the blesser, the dignified movements of a balanced person, the jerky ones of a nervous person, all speak their own language.

Physiognomy, or the science of expression, must give an intelligent interpretation of all this. Of course there are limits, and some things that are inexplicable. Max Picard has made a thorough study of the human face. He points out that only in an animal's face does every feature correspond, i.e. look exactly as you would expect with regard to any other part. Animals are bound by nature's laws; man has a certain freedom. The pike's eye looks as greedy as its mouth. This may also be the case with a man but not necessarily so. The animal fits into its world harmoniously and therefore is widely predictable. Man has two sides to his nature and is out of harmony with his world. He is therefore unpredictable. That is where physiognomy meets its limit.

In addition to this fundamental consideration, it should be pointed out that most palmists, even such sound ones as Hugo Steindamm and Elsbeth Ackermann, expect too much from a study of the hands. Basically, physiognomy can only record a man's character *statically*, i.e. state that he has such and such qualities, and even if his strivings, instinctive urges and spiritual conflicts are recognisable, it is only superficially. To penetrate the inner being of a man we must turn to psychology. In its modern forms of psychoanalysis and depth psychology, it tells us about his present and past existence at any given moment. To give a picture of a man's character is, therefore, a difficult undertaking. In principle there are no methods which give a quick and reliable result.

All this is very true when we turn to palmistry which is mixed up with a lot of mythological, cabbalistic and astrological ideas. For example, astrology assigns a planet to each finger. As there were seven planets and only five fingers, Mars and the Moon had to be content with so-called "mountains" formed by the elevations on the palm of the hand. Once you have established a fanciful scheme of this kind, you can draw definite conclusions which, none-the-less, are pure speculations without any foundation in fact. Thus you find in Issberner-Haldane's book *Scientific Palmistry*, "If the Jupiter finger is very long, it shows a great preference for religion. When it is as long as the Saturn finger, it means your life is dominated by ambition. A very long Saturn finger, on the other hand, indicates trickery and frivolity."

It is nonsensical to maintain that the lines of the hand can be labelled head-line, heart-line, profession-line and so on. The most you can say is that all the lines of the hand give some general information about a man's character. The lines of Einstein's hands show clarity and broadmindedness. A confusion of small lines criss-crossing each other indicates a small-minded man who is not clear in his thinking. But what a medley of *stars* and *crosses* is read from even the smallest crossings in the lines of the hands!

Itinerant palmists who often enjoy a very wide clientele, try to read from the lifeline the main events of individual lives such as illness, advancement, marriage and so on. That is superstition, the same superstition that is practised by the *iris diagnosers* who believe that all diseases can be diagnosed from a certain definite list of signs without any understanding of the person or medical knowledge (Diagram 13). It is possible that this life line, which exists only on human hands and is formed by the juxtaposition of the thumb and fingers, may have something to do with the

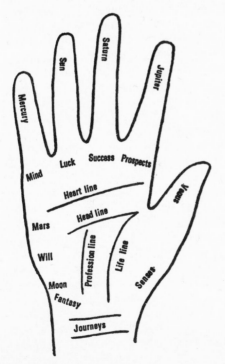

Diag. 13
Superstitious interpretation of the hand.

154

vitality of the person. It can never be a short résumé of his whole life. Mixing this up with astrology produces some amusing results. The Uranus, or intuition-line, means intuition, insight and possibly light-headedness. The Neptune, or poison-line, if it is there at all and extends from the lower Venus mountain, or middle of the hand, to the middle or upper Moon mountain, indicates presence of medicinal poisons in the body and sorrows of mistaken love. The theological writings of Ursula von Mangoldt suffer from this mixture of astrology and unfounded superstitions.

We do hear, however, from time to time that a palmist has been right and has even foretold the future correctly. Stories of gypsies who have forecast a divorce or an accident accurately have often been related. But after what has gone before there is no need to explain how such lucky shots come about. A combination of detailed knowledge, deception of memory, suggestion and urge for fulfilment often forms a kind of *syndrome*, a concurrence or *tangle of phenomena* (Bender), which is hard to unravel. So it comes about that the hand, like the divining rod or the horoscope can be used as a *shaft* for descending into the unconscious and performing an act of an abnormal nature like telepathy or second sight, and using all the truth but also all the dangerous elements that we have already mentioned.

A man of faith will not entrust his hand, his destiny nor his future to a gypsy or a palmist. He will rather trust Him of whom he may say, "My times are in His hands" (Psalm 31:16).

12

The Task of the Church

IN taking stock of superstition and occult phenomena, we have
covered a wide field. It extends from extremely foolish, though
harmless ideas, to the evils of magic: from cold-blooded exploita-
tion of human stupidity to the cramping and decadence of spiritual life: from fantasy and swindle to remarkable paranormal
ability and achievement.

The task with which we are faced by all this complexity will
be threefold:

1. Purely scientific. This will engage in all possible research
and seek to distinguish between the true and the false. It consists in finding rational explanations as far as possible and fitting
the phenomena into the other branches of science. That is what
parapsychology aims to do. It is a young science and must be
prepared to break through the hitherto accepted limits set by the
natural sciences whenever new evidence makes that necessary.

2. Medical psychotherapy. The doctor faces people suffering
from superstition or hallucinations, not only as an investigator
but also as a healer who tries to restore the sick person to
normal, healthy life.

3. The Church and the Christian community. This is the most
important of the three. Christians must lead people who are the
slaves of evil spirits and occult practices into a new life of faith,
and with God's help, bring them into a liberating experience of
Christ's power to set them free.

Christians will be glad to co-operate with the scientists in
their task. Educational lectures and books are always useful and
have an effect on reasonable minds. For example, astronomers
endeavour by talks and television programmes to give a realistic
picture of what is happening in the star world. In this way they
disabuse people's minds of the false notions of the astrologers.

But by itself this has proved inadequate. Those who believe
in the stars look at their horoscope, not from a rational point
of view, but out of a desire to know the future or out of fear
for themselves. Fritz Künkel has given a good example of the

weakness of purely rational enlightenment. An independent businessman, thirty-five years old, had become so shy and anxious that he was no longer any use for work. After the therapeutist had, as he thought, cleared away several of his inhibitions through frank discussion, the patient brought out his horoscope and *proved* from the opposition of Mars and Saturn, and the very unfavourable position of the moon, that he was incurable. The doctor refrained from giving him a lecture on the valueless nature of astrology. He recognised that this was just another attempt at escape on the part of the patient. Instead he went into the horoscope thoroughly and pointed out a favourable position of Jupiter which rendered the opposition ineffective. The patient then put away his horoscope and never mentioned it again. If anyone had tried to call astrology the work of the devil or foolish superstition, he would only have added to the patient's readiness to take refuge in the horoscope again.

The system of connection in astrology is often only a barricade behind which men seek to hide from the conflicts and sufferings of life. The therapeutist's aim, on the other hand, is to show that no system of thought or philosophy of the world can absolve a man from taking responsibility for his life and bearing the consequences of his decisions. It is possible in this matter, to misuse one's Christian beliefs. Instead of surrendering his life to God, he may use orthodox belief to become his own protector and the centre of his life. It was to counter this that Jesus told the parable of the Pharisee and the Publican (Luke 18:9 ff.).

Thus we see that rational explanation does not get to the roots of a man's reliance on superstition. It often rejects genuinely abnormal phenomena and in that way only arouses fresh opposition in the people concerned. Aided by the methods of depth psychology and medicine we can go further and deeper. The Church may well be grateful for the advances made in the last hundred years in our knowledge of human nature and the new methods of healing that have resulted. Every pastor, and that means every adult Christian who takes his responsibility seriously, should learn something of depth psychology and therapeutics. The theological student should also take this into account and be trained by specialists in the practical study of man's nature, particularly his psychic illnesses. This should not be designed to lead to what Thurney has called a "dangerous dilettantism" but should show the future pastor where his limits are and where he should leave things to the doctor.

If three years' extra study is required to train a doctor in psychotherapy, how presumptious it would be to try to help and heal without expert knowledge! Where it is a matter of definite neuroses or psychoses a specialist is essential. No amount of faith can make up for a pastor's ignorance.

This is a sound rule. If a pastor does perform a miracle and overcomes all the complexities it is because he is full of grace. Above all it is a rare, exceptional case and not his work, but that of the incomprehensible and merciful Spirit of God. Doctors and pastors ought to co-operate a great deal more than they do today and learn from each other. The pastor will then find out from the doctor how slow and arduous is the work of healing the mentally sick.

One must consider too that the doctor, in his capacity of healer, is at the same time usually a scientist. His domain is the immanent world and his success in healing is thereby limited to it. He can indeed succeed in reintegrating a nerve-ridden, anti-social person into society and help him to meet his responsibilities. He can help also to clear away a whole series of complexes and wrong ideas. He knows about the relationship between illness and feelings of guilt and he need not be ignorant of the part religion plays. C. G. Jung records that all his patients over the age of thirty-five had a religious complex. For him religion was the projection of the psyche outwards.

In the realm of the transcendental, where man may meet God, only faith can lead. Here the doctor has no power to set men free. It is a gift of God's grace and is met with in church circles. The Christian doctor can prepare his patients for it and also be a pastor. Many modern practitioners in therapeutics, like Alphons Maeder, Paul Tournier or Fritz Künkel come near to being this. "We human beings," says Künkel, "can only remove hindrances. We cannot effect the cure. The real healing, i.e. reconciliation with God and forgiveness of sin, is a miracle from above. In this the experience of science coincides with the teaching of Christianity: 'Change comes through grace'."

The psychotherapist is then able to help an inhibited person back to normal life in society. But Christians know that the normal man, the citizen, the conscientious official and the model mother are all sinners in the sight of God, i.e. are separated from Him until He has mercy on them and enters into fellowship with them again. And we know that the sin of sins is to have no faith at all or to believe in superstition. In either case man wants to separate himself from God and live as his own master. He becomes in fact a God-substitute. Genuine pastoral work is concerned with giving people a faith and so finds itself in a different sphere from psychotherapy and needs different practitioners, but as we have seen a combination of the two is what we should aim at.

We must now consider certain points that are of particular importance for the pastoral care of those who are in the grip of superstition or are enthusiastic worshippers of occult phenomena.

1. We must have courage and give time and love to the individual. One or two talks are not sufficient. If psychotherapy requires dozens of sessions spread over five or six months to cure a neurosis, we shall not need less time to clear away the fences and opposition people put up; and we must be patient. If I have guidance from God that He wants me to help a man, I must have the courage to let other things go. Christ recommended that we should leave the ninety-nine sheep and go after the lost one. What use is it to say a few words of help and then hurry away?

A fifty-nine-year-old woman came to see me with her husband. She described the state of anxiety which kept overcoming her, though she knew it was foolish. A fortune-teller had declared that she would die in her sixtieth year. It is obvious that in this case only a continual contact could help, especially as other events the fortune-teller had foretold, had actually happened. "Faith is a means of removing dangerous suggestions," says Paul Tournier and recounts how a woman who felt she was laid under a curse recovered her inner freedom through faith and prayer.

2. Something more than the healer's effort is needed. The patient must also co-operate. This he does when he has the courage to confess. Even in Protestant churches confession is taking a more important place. In our pastoral work it seems to be an absolute necessity. A formal and solemn renunciation of the devil before witnesses is regarded by Koch and others as essential for any cure from his spell. In spite of the objection that the patient might think that this was another form of magic, I think the pastors are right. They know from experience that such help is needed. Even for normal Christians who may nourish a secret belief in superstition, a frank and free confession can be valuable.

A young man wrote to tell me that he had become happily engaged. He was particularly grateful for the love his fiancée was giving him, as he was a cripple. They had then had their horoscope read and he had broken off their engagement without telling her why. It was a shattering blow. His horoscope said their marriage would be extremely unhappy and his sufferings would get worse and worse! I advised him not only to burn the paper, but to tell her what he had done and ask her forgiveness for his lack of trust in her. With the young man's consent, I informed his own pastor. Now I hear that the shadows cast by the horoscope have disappeared.

3. We must, furthermore, learn Jesus's prescription for preparing to exercise pastoral care—prayer and fasting (Mark 9: 29) and take it more seriously. It must be not just intermittent prayer, but a life of prayer, of daily intercession for people by name. Fasting must not be just an ascetic discipline for the achievement of perfection of the soul, but a genuine renunciation in order to have strength and time for the person in danger. We saw how Blumhardt expended himself night and day for weeks to cure Gottliebin Dittus.

4. In this pastoral work we cannot do much by individual effort. The person who believes in superstition is self-centred and needs to be brought into the fellowship of a community who pray and study the Bible. We pastors multiply our power when we are sustained by such a community. This is true of every parson. He should not be above asking his people to help him with prayer in the church or in his house or even with the patient he is trying to help. That was how it was done in the early church (Jas. 5: 14). Getting the affected person into a happy and healthy family has often worked wonders.

5. We must not forget the power of the sacraments. The people we want to help are enslaved by subconscious inhibitions. The sacrament is the visible sign of a power that works below the surface more deeply than we realise. God uses His healing power in the sacraments of Baptism and the Lord's Supper without the expenditure of many words, but it must be made patently clear that we are not engaging in another magical practice. Beelzebub cannot cast out devils! That is why we have only made cautious reference to the early Christian practice of laying on of hands, anointing with oil or exorcism.

6. Participation in confession should, as far as possible, be followed up by what Bodelschwingh called "work therapy". The convert should be found some job in the church community, however small. With converted diviners and fortune-tellers one should not be afraid to send them to their former companions with a reliable Christian and let them discuss the matter with them. It will strengthen their new convictions.

7. Finally we must face the fact that there are many among our Christian communities who still believe in superstition. We have seen already that good mothers and kindergarten and Sunday school teachers often implant a fear of demons in the minds of their children. We should deal very carefully and thoughtfully

with the second commandment when instructing children in religion and preparing them for confirmation. We must be neither too rational nor too irrational about it. Steep and narrow is the path between unbelief and superstition.

In many good Christian families you find people who have their horoscope to tell them about their future, and quack medicines are still believed in. A parson's wife had an apparatus against earth rays under her bed to ward off sleepless nights. The matron of a deaconess' home taps on wood or says "touch wood" when asked about her health. Some still use the Bible as an oracle to make up their minds for them.

This all goes to show how much we need to pray as did the father whose son was given to having fits, "Lord I believe; help Thou my unbelief!" (Mark 9: 24) and we might add, "my superstition".

May God in His mercy grant us the right faith which does not seek to command happiness through magical practices or formulae, nor to be curious about the future, nor to penetrate beyond the confines of death, nor desire a miracle of healing as the aim of life; which does not ask the stars for God's will, nor needs any occult rituals to bring us nearer to God. May He give us the faith He gave Jesus Christ through the Holy Spirit to fear, love and trust Him alone, above all else!

So now my soul be His
And trust in Him alone
Who hath created thee.
For all things that may come,
Thy Father from above
Thy Counsellor will be.